FREE WILL
AND FOUR ENGLISH
PHILOSOPHERS (HOBBES
LOCK, HUME AND MILL)

FREE WILL

AND FOUR ENGLISH PHILO-SOPHERS.· (HOBBES, LOCKE HUME AND MILL)·BY THE REV. JOSEPH RICKABY, S.J.

"The belief in freedom is at the root of our entire conception of personality "
—*Mallock, Reconstruction of Belief*

Essay Index Reprint Series

BOOKS FOR LIBRARIES PRESS
FREEPORT, NEW YORK

First Published 1906
Reprinted 1969

STANDARD BOOK NUMBER:
8369-1103-2

LIBRARY OF CONGRESS CATALOG CARD NUMBER:
74-84333

PRINTED IN THE UNITED STATES OF AMERICA

THE PREFACE

IN their original form these pages were written in the years 1871-4. Since then they have been submitted to much castigation and amendment, less perhaps than they deserve, at the hands of the writer, then youthful, now an elderly man. This fact may account for some inequalities of style. Certain "tender memories of the past" have stayed my hand from pruning away all traces of the exuberance of youth.

Meanwhile the importance of the subject has grown rather than diminished, chiefly, I think, owing to the prevalence of the Kantian philosophy. I may as well forewarn the reader that Kant is not discussed here, except indirectly, in so far as the phenomenalism of Hume may be considered to have prepared the way for Kant. I have written elsewhere: "Though men are slow to see it and loth to own it,—from reminiscences I think of the *odium theologicum* hanging about the question,—free will still remains the hub and centre of philosophical speculation." * In this work the subject is treated entirely on philosophical grounds: that is to say, there is no reference to grace, predestination, or the Fall. Thus St Augustine stands out of the controversy: so too Calvin and Jansenius. My

* "Free Will in God and Man," pp. 142-155, in the Second Series of my *Oxford and Cambridge Conferences*, 1900-1901: see also in my *Political and Moral Essays*, 1902, an Essay on "Morality without Free Will."

method is to quote a passage from the English philosopher under examination, and then discuss it. The method has its drawbacks, but it ensures definiteness, and seems about as fair to the philosopher discussed as any other form of procedure. It is not the writer's fault if the reader has not his Hobbes, or his Locke, or his Hume by his side, and does not read round and study in the context the extract presented to him.

The *fact* that man has free will is far more certain, —it is a point of Catholic faith,—than any explanation *how* he has it. As to how free will works, the Church has given no explanation: there is much divergence even of orthodox opinion, and, wherever my reading has travelled, considerable obscurity. The fact is usually proved by the indirect method of enlarging upon the consequences of a denial of free will. That method I too have frequently employed. But further I offer some positive view of the precise working of free will. I have not borrowed it from Locke. I arrived at the view, or rather was led into it, in the year 1868; and it has satisfied my mind ever since. It will be found, however, to approximate to a view put forward, on second thoughts, by Locke.* The view I take is briefly this. To will at all, our will must be struck by a motive, which raises in us what I have have called a "spontaneous complacency." As the four philosophers under review all agree, and I agree with them, this complacency is a fact of physical sequence, a necessity, under the circumstances. But it is not yet a volition. It does not become a volition until it is

* See Extract 8 from Locke, pp. 100-104.

hugged, embraced, enhanced, under advertence, by
the conscious self. This process takes time,—I do not
mean so many seconds measured by the watch, for
thought time goes on other wheels than motion time,
—but still it takes time. Free will turns upon the
absence of any need of your making up your mind
at once to accept the particular complacency thus present in your soul: observe, you cannot here and now
accept any other; you cannot here and now accept
what is not here and now offered; you cannot just at
present fling yourself upon the absent. Thus time is
gained for rival motives to come up, according to the
ordinary laws of association, perception, or personal
intercourse: each of these motives excites its own
necessary complacency, till at last some present complacency is accepted and endorsed by the person; and
that is an act of free will. Not to have a *regressus in infinitum*, we must further observe that no volition is
requisite simply to hesitate, delay, and withhold your
acceptance of any present complacency,—in fact, to remain undecided and irresolute. You may, of course, put
forth a positive volition to wait and see more of the
question: all I say is that such a positive volition is
not indispensable; your will may hang fire without
your resolving to be irresolute: which important point
Locke never came clearly to remark.

This explanation may not account for free will in
God and in His holy angels; but in so difficult a matter
it is much if we can form some theory which a philosopher may debate, and a sound theologian will not
bar as "heretical," "erroneous," or "temerarious."

I may add that while I am much concerned that my reader should not be a determinist, I am comparatively indifferent whether he accepts my explanation of free will, or any other, or regards the process as inexplicable.   J. R.

Pope's Hall, Oxford,
Midsummer, 1906.

THE CONTENTS

THOMAS HOBBES

JOHN LOCKE

DAVID HUME

THE CONTENTS xj

FREE WILL
AND FOUR ENGLISH PHILOSOPHERS

THOMAS HOBBES

Of Liberty and Necessity: a Treatise wherein all Controversy concerning Predestination, Election, Free Will, Grace, Merits, Reprobation, etc., is fully decided and cleared: in answer to a Treatise written by the Bishop of Londonderry on the same subject

I

"WHEREAS he says thus, If I be free to write this discourse, I have obtained the cause; I deny that to be true, for it is enough to his freedom of writing that he had not written it, unless he would himself. . . . It may be his Lordship [the Bishop] thinks it all one to say, I was free to write it, and, It was not necessary I should write it. But I think otherwise. For he is free to do a thing, that may do it if he have the will to do it; and may forbear if he have the will to forbear. And yet if there be a necessity that he shall have the will to do it, the action is necessarily to follow; and if there be a necessity that he shall have the will to forbear, the forbearing also will be necessary. The question therefore is not, whether a man be a free agent, that is to say, whether he can write or forbear, speak

or be silent, according to his will; but whether the will
to write and the will to forbear come upon him according to his will or according to anything else in his own
power, I acknowledge this liberty that I can do if I
will; but to say I can will if I will I take to be an
absurd speech."

Hobbes considers human agency to be at once free
and necessitated: free, because the action follows the
will of the agent; necessitated, inasmuch as the agent,
under the circumstances, could not possibly have willed
otherwise than as he did will.

Hobbes takes it to be an absurd speech to say I can
will if I will. What indeed is the meaning of that
phrase in the mouths of such as use it? An outline of
what they mean would run thus: Upon adverting to
a present affection, a like or a dislike which has risen
up within me, I am often competent either to take up
or not to take up that affection: if I do take it up, I
elicit a volition or full act of my will, which is a free act
inasmuch as I take up, adopt and sanction for my own
an affection which I am competent not to sanction;
while for my sanctioning it no reason can be given beyond the fact that I, a person, that is an intelligent
nature, exerting my privilege as a person, do choose to
lend myself to the affection which has come over me.

An example. An opportunity offers for striking a lu-
orative but unjust bargain. The idea recurs of securing
the gain, and my breast warms with approbetion of that
idea. So far I have been the passive victim of associations and feelings. There has been no personal action
emanating from me. I now advert to my mind's spon-

taneous and unauthorised approval of this idea. If I continue to approve of it under advertence, spontaneity passes into freedom, the movement started from without has been sustained from within me. I have willed that which at first I felt. But perhaps I do not decide quite so readily. I let feelings and the ideas which occasion them troop in associated trains across the stage of my consciousness. I retain none of them. Conflicting thoughts of gain and of honesty, the joys of a good bargain, the remorses of a fraud, replace one another, as past mental experience marshals their array. Whilst this process lasts, I am said to be thinking the matter over. At length my mind is made up. The idea of improving the opportunity or else the idea of letting the opportunity pass has recurred: it has given me complacency, as it gave me before, and this time I have embraced the complacency. Thereby I have done a voluntary act. I may indeed recall it, but still it is done. And the act, besides being voluntary, is free, for in it I have embraced a complacency which I need not have embraced.

The above is a mere statement of doctrine, not a proof. But surely it is something to state clearly a doctrine which adversaries pronounce nonsensical. Nonsense generally will not bear stating. If, then, I have presented an intelligible, definite theory, there is presumption of its not being nonsense.

Great part of the discredit that attaches to the doctrine of free will comes from its being supposed to mean that whatever a man may do from morning to night he does everything alike freely. Nothing of the sort. A reflective adult performs perhaps a dozen actions a day that are altogether free: a child,—whether a child proper or a grown baby,—say half a dozen: call another hundred actions free more or less, and you may describe the rest of the man's daily course as shaped without advertence and without freedom, except such part of it as is determined by previous free acts. That part would be technically termed free in its cause. The freedom of an agent bears a direct ratio to his actual knowledge of what he is about: now as mankind know what they are about, some more, some less, some scarcely at all, and none always with an actual knowledge, it cannot be said that all the actions of men are free, or that all their free actions are equally free.

Much light falls on this matter from the counsels of Christian ascetics. Let me point in passing to the splendid psychological education which the Church presses upon her children, teaching them to lead an interior life, to examine their consciences, to confess their sins not of word and deed only, but also sins of thought. These Christian spiritualists, then, warn us against doing our actions through routine and custom, telling us that we shall gain little merit by such mechanical performances. Why little merit? Because merit attaches to conscious agents, not to automata; to freedom, not to machinery. A creature of habit, working blindly in a secondarily automatic groove, may be a useful machine, but scarcely a virtuous man. At the same time we learn from the above-cited authorities that a general pious intention not revoked suffices to impart merit to a long sequence of work gone through with-

out further advertence. This instruction clears away
a difficulty that is often urged against our freedom.
How, it is asked, can that human action be free which
may be unerringly calculated beforehand to be about
to occur? "When a commander orders his soldiers to
wheel, to deploy, to form square, to fire a battery,"*
Mr Samuel Bailey demands, "is he less confident in
the result than he is when he performs some physical
operation,—when he draws a sword, pulls a trigger, or
seals a dispatch?" Supposing that he is equally confident of both results, still I say the physical result is
a sheer necessity, while the moral result is due to a
foregone free volition. Those soldiers declare their will
once for all to wheel, deploy, form square, or fire a battery at the word of command. They willed when they
need not have willed to undertake these manœuvres.
They may be conscripts, but they are not dummies;
they took their allotted service freely. They were not
brought into the ranks like sacks of stones: they came
there, and no one could have foretold for certain that
such and such men individually would consent to
come. But once they have come, their officers calculate upon that general intention of obedience of which
the uniform is a pledge. The soldier need not will to
obey for every order he executes: his initial purpose is
enough, if he does not depart from it. But so to depart would require an express new volition, as obedience is in possession. A volition, however, does not
spring up without a motive. If then an officer has no
ground to imagine any motive for mutiny rife amongst

* *Letters on the Philosophy of the Human Mind*, second series, p. 166.

his men, he relies upon their previous loyal purpose working itself out unopposed; and he feels as sure of their muscles as they of their powder.

It is further to be observed that a perfect apparent good,—or in other words, a good which quite satisfies him to whom it occurs,—does not leave the will the liberty of refusing. But such a perfect good hardly ever presents itself to an adult who adverts to what he enjoys. The psalmist sings, "Take delight in the LORD." Undoubtedly the LORD fills with delight the blessed souls who "see Him as He is"; but He seldom satisfies our capacity for delight, who see Him "in a glass, darkly." Therefore the delight which we consciously take in the LORD is free, and if free also meritorious. It is our present sore distress, and at the same time the condition of our merit and eternal reward, that the ability to conceive enjoyment in us vastly transcends our ability to enjoy. Take any enjoyment that you can: think of it, and your thought has outrun it; you want more. There are rare moments when some unexpected blessing received fills our heart brimming over: nothing seems wanting then to our bliss but continuance. But the very names of rapture, transport, ecstasy applied to such states show that in these states feeling momentarily precludes reflection. We are not free in those moments: no mind is free without reflection. But when "Richard is himself again," when we reflect upon our state, forthwith we conceive something better and our liberty of choice returns. By our use of liberty we make our way to our lasting city. There we shall gaze face to face on perfect goodness, and yield for eternity

our feeling, our understanding and our will to the
sweet constraints of His love. Till then "content is
not the natural frame of any human mind, but is the
offspring of compromise."*

II

"All voluntary actions, where the thing that indu-
ceth the will is not fear, are called also spontaneous. . .
But every spontaneous action is not therefore voluntary, for voluntary presupposes some precedent deliberation. . . His Lordship is deceived, if he think
any spontaneous action, after once being checked in
it, differs from an action voluntary and elective; for
even the setting of a man's foot in the posture for
walking, and the action of ordinary eating, was once
deliberated of how and when it should be done; and
though afterwards it became easy and habitual so as to
be done without forethought, yet that does not hinder
but that the act is voluntary and proceedeth from
election."

A *voluntary* action Hobbes defines to be a premeditated action: a *spontaneous* action he defines to be any
action, premeditated or unpremeditated, that is not dictated by fear. He continues: Once we have stopped
over a spontaneous action, and thought in the act how
we should do it, every subsequent spontaneous repetition, besides being spontaneous, is also a premeditated or voluntary action. Whence he concludes against
the Bishop,—who had laid it down that spontaneous
actions were necessary, voluntary actions free,—that an
action may be spontaneous and voluntary at the same

* Bain's *Emotions and Will*, p. 453.

time, in other words, "that *necessity* and *election* may stand together."

I cannot think that Bishop Bramhall, when he called spontaneous actions necessitated actions, classed as spontaneous all actions not dictated by fear. That is Hobbes's account of the word *spontaneous*. But had it been the Bishop's, he would never have written against Hobbes in defence of free will, for, allowing that actions not dictated by fear were necessitated, he could not possibly pretend that actions dictated by fear were free; so that, between actions done for fear and actions not done for fear, all actions whatsoever would be done of necessity; that is, the Bishop would have agreed with Hobbes.

Surely, too, it is a strange argument that habitual actions are premeditated, because the actions, which formed the habit, were premeditated. Consider the habit of dancing. A pupil curveting for the first time before a dancing-master studies every step. But to declare in consequence that, when the pupil has become an expert, every trip of his "light fantastic toe" in the ballroom is a premeditated action,—this surely is either an abuse of reason or an abuse of language. If Hobbes means by "premeditated" what ordinary Englishmen mean, namely, "done with forethought," then his conclusion does not follow from his premisses; but if he means "formerly done with forethought," he must be speaking some other language than English. I allow that the resolution to dance at a ball is a premeditated voluntary act, but I refuse to extend the appellation to each step which the dancer takes. It is upon such habitual operations* that the issue raised by Hobbes turns.

* Called by physiologists "secondarily automatic movements." Dr Carpenter says: "There can be no doubt that the nerve-force is disposed to pass in special *tracks;* and it seems probable that while some of these are originally marked out for the automatic movements, others [i.e., the nerve-tracks of the secondarily automatic movements] may be gradually worn in, so to say, by the habitual actions of the will; and that when a train of sequential actions primarily directed by the will has once been set in operation, it may continue without any further influence from that source. . . An individual who is subject to 'absence of mind,' may fall into a reverie whilst walking in the streets; his attention may be entirely absorbed in a train of thought, and he may be utterly unconscious of any interruption in its continuity; and yet during the whole of that time his limbs shall have been in motion, carrying him along the accustomed path. . . It has been maintained by some metaphysicians and physiologists, that these 'secondarily automatic' movements always continue to be voluntary, because their performance is originally due to a succession of volitional acts, and because, in any particular case, it is the will which first excites them, whilst an exertion of the will serves to check them at any time. But this doctrine involves the notion that the will is in a state of pendulum-like oscillation between the train of thought and the train of movement; whereas nothing is more certain to the individual who is the subject of both, than that the former may be as uninterrupted as if the body were perfectly at rest, and his reverie were taking place in the quietude of his own study. And as it commonly happens that the direction taken is that in which the individual is most in the habit of walking, it will not unfrequently occur that if he had previously intended to pursue some other, he finds himself, when his reverie is at an end, in a locality which may be very remote from that towards which his walk was originally destined; which would not be the case if his movements had been still under the purposive direction of the will. And although it is perfectly true that these movements can be at any time checked by an effort of the will, yet this does not really indicate that the will has been previously engaged in sustaining them; since, for the will to act upon them at all, the *attention*

Hobbes has used his own terminology, and not his adversary's. I crave permission to do likewise. By a *spontaneous act* of the will, then, I understand the complacency which arises from the apprehension of good, previous to advertence. This spontaneous act is a necessary act. By a *voluntary* act I understand the adhesion with advertence to a complacency. That act of complacency, from being spontaneous, becomes voluntary by being consciously adhered to. If the complacency does not quite satisfy him who is the subject of it, and yet he adheres to it, then his voluntary act is *free*, he adheres where he need not. But if the complacency under advertence does quite satisfy him, he cannot but adhere; his adhesion then is an act at once voluntary and necessary. Therefore voluntariness and necessity may stand together, as Hobbes argued they might. But it does not follow that they commonly do stand together in this world.

III

"That which I say necessitateth and determinateth every action, is the sum of all things, which being now existent, conduce and concur to the production of that action hereafter, whereof if any one thing now were wanting, the effect could not be produced."

A special interest attaches to this extract: for if we read *phenomena* in place of *things*, and *infallibly deter-*

---

must be recalled to them, and the cerebrum must be liberated from its previous self-occupation." The same authority terms the formation of a secondarily automatic habit, "the gradual conversion of a volitional into an automatic train of movements, so that at last this train, once started, shall continue to run down of itself."—*Principles of Human Physiology*, pp. 592, 610, seventh edition.

minateth for *necessitateth and determinateth*, those slight amendments will bring Hobbes exactly to express a view very generally taken at the present day regarding causation both physical and mental.

For an instance of physical causation we will consider the orbit of the earth. I will enumerate "the sum of all things which being now existent conduce and concur to the production of that action, whereof if any one thing now were wanting, the effect could not be produced." There are the sun and the remaining planets; item, the distance of the earth from each of the other planets and from the sun; item, the tangential velocity of the earth; item, the respective masses of earth, sun and planets; item, the absence of further perturbatory influences, such as would arise from the introduction of a new member into the solar system. Were any part of this enumeration left out, and no compensation given, "the effect could not be produced," i.e., the earth would not then describe the path which it does describe under its present data.*

* The absence of influences that might have been present in a particular case, but are not, need not be specified in the Hobbesian view. All history being an unbroken chain of consequent following antecedent,—"necessarily," according to Hobbes, "uniformly," according to Mill,—pure possibility, or "that which might be but never shall," becomes a name of nothing. "Every act which is possible shall at some time be produced" (Hobbes, *First Grounds of Philosophy*, chap. ix). Therefore to talk of what might have been, how, for instance, an effect which has followed from one cause might have followed from another, "I take to be an absurd speech." To the best of our previous knowledge, the effect might have followed from another cause; but now that it has followed from this, we know that could not have followed from aught else. Modern Nominalists, perceiving that if *could* means *did*, then *could not* means *did not*,

The older philosophers would distinguish among the enumerated determinants of the orbit aforesaid. The attracting bodies they would style the "causes," but the disposition of those bodies in space, along with the absence of perturbation, they would style the "conditions" of the particular effect observable in that orbit. And they would define *cause*, "the thing which acts"; and *conditions*, "the circumstances under which a cause acts." The modern school, however, of which Hobbes was a forerunner, applies the name *condition* to "each of the things which produce and concur to the production of that action," and denominates the "sum" of those things the "cause" of the action or effect produced. "The cause," says Mill,* "is the sum total of the conditions, positive and negative, taken together." If one of these conditions were wanting, and were not otherwise supplied, the effect could not be produced. Their "sum," in Hobbesian phrase, "necessitateth and determinateth" the effect. Mill, eschewing all mention of necessity, would say, "Their sum causes the effect"; meaning, "they are the set of antecedents,

have struck out of their philosophical vocabulary the superfluous expressions, *can, could, might, must, power, possibility, necessity.* This cancelling of terms alone differentiates the "uniformist" from the "necessarian," John Stuart Mill from Thomas Hobbes. Under this *caveat* we must read the phrase, "plurality of causes," where it occurs in Mill's writings; not that one and the same effect could follow wholly from each of many causes, but that like effects have followed from many causes; whence the inadmissibility of the bare argument from effect to cause. I subjoin this note because I wish to show how little ultimate difference there is between Hobbes and the modern thinkers with whom I am about to compare him.

* *Logic*, bk iii, chap. v, § 3.

positive and negative, upon which the consequent invariably follows without further condition."

For moral causation let us revert to our example of a man being tempted to strike a bargain, advantageous but unjust. Suppose he yields. Let us sift out and distinguish cause and condition in that free act. The cause of the volition is the man himself. He, and no other thing besides, causes the volition, full and free. But he is not the cause of the initial complacency, or the original impulse to do wrong. That complacency resulted in him necessarily and inevitably from the news which he heard, supervening upon his previous habits of mind. But, upon reflection, the object of this complacency proves to be not all that he could wish. The mere moral turpitude of the thing is a volitional drawback. This inadequacy of the object to his thinking mind leaves him free: he may either sustain the complacency into which he finds himself spontaneously thrown, and so sustaining it pour himself out and identify himself with the object, or he may let it pass. If he so sustains his spontaneous complacency, he freely wills, and that under the following conditions, remote and proximate. The proximate condition is the impulsive complacency which, like the wash of a steamer, went along with the idea of the bargain, when that idea, uninvited, entered his mind. The facts reported to him, and his antecedent views of a good bargain, were the remote conditions giving rise to the complacency. But his openeyed acceptance of the complacency without thorough contentment in the same,—in other words, the free act of his will,—is chargeable on himself alone. He caused it, he did it, he is answerable for it,—he, and not his circumstances.

IV

"The will itself, and each propension of a man during his deliberation, is as much necessitated, and depends on a sufficient cause as anything else whatsoever."

Hobbes, in another work, explains what he means by a "sufficient," or "entire," cause.

"The aggregate of accidents in the agent or agents, requisite for the production of the effect, the effect being produced, is called the efficient cause thereof; and the aggregate of accidents in the patient, the effect being produced, is usually called the material cause. . . . But the efficient and material causes are both but partial causes, or parts of that cause, which in the next precedent article I called an entire cause. . . In whatsoever instant the cause is entire, in the same instant the effect is produced. For if it be not produced, something is still wanting which is requisite for the production of it; and therefore the cause was not entire, as was supposed. And seeing a necessary cause is defined to be that, which being supposed, the effect cannot but follow, this also may be collected, that whatsoever effect is produced at any time, the same is produced by a necessary cause. For whatsoever is produced, inasmuch as it is produced, had an entire cause, that is, had all those things, which being supposed, it cannot be understood but that the effect follows; that is, it had a necessary cause. And in the same manner it may be shown that whatsoever effects are hereafter to be produced shall have a necessary cause; so that all the effects that have been, or shall be produced, have their necessity in things antecedent."*

Admitting that the act of will "depends on a sufficient cause," I deny that "it is as much necessitated as anything else whatsoever." I deny that "in whatsoever instant the cause is entire, in the same instant the effect is produced"; likewise that "whatsoever effect is produced at any time, the same is produced by a necessary cause." In short, I deny that a sufficient (or entire) cause and a necessary cause are the same. Every cause is in a certain sense entire; it is entire as a cause. Such entirety would still appertain to the sun, were there no planets to suffer the solar attraction. But that an entire and sufficient cause may work an actual effect, certain conditions are requisite. Hobbes takes an "entire cause" to be an agent surrounded with the conditions of action, for instance, a planet having a satellite within range. I say that the planet is an entire cause by itself, irrespectively of any satellite. But waiving

* Cf. "The state of the whole universe at any instant we believe to be the consequence of its state at the previous instant; insomuch that one who knew all the agents which exist at the present moment, their collocation in space, and all their properties, in other words, the laws of their agency, could predict the whole subsequent history of the universe, at least unless some new volition of a power capable of controlling the universe should supervene. And if any particular state of the entire universe could ever recur a second time, all subsequent states would return too, and history would, like a circulating decimal of many figures, periodically repeat itself:

Jam redit et Virgo, redeunt Saturnia regna. . .
Alter erit tum Tiphys, et altera quæ vehit Argo
Delectos heroas; erunt quoque altera bella,
Atque iterum ad Trojam magnus mittetur Achilles."
—Mill, *Logic*, bk iii, ch. v, § 7.

that definition, and allowing 'entire and sufficient cause'
to mean 'a cause so conditioned that it may be followed by its effect without further condition,' or 'that,
which being supposed, the effect can follow'; and fur-
thermore accepting Hobbes's definition of 'necessary
cause' as "that, which being supposed, the effect cannot but follow"; still, I must protest against the equi-
valence of *can follow* and *cannot but follow;* and, consequently, I cannot allow that every sufficient cause in
the Hobbesian sense of that term is at the same time
a necessary cause. Every sufficient mechanical cause is
necessary; but a mental cause may be sufficient and
yet not necessary. How so? Precisely by this,—that
matter is ruled wholly from without, but mind par-
tially from within. Matter is carried here and there,
dependent on external causes and their collocation:
whereas the liability of mind to be led captive by a
foreign power stops short at the point where mind
begins to think and to reflect, and thence to choose for
itself.

V

"He who forces another to do a thing, and then
punishes him for doing of the same, is unjust (according to the common sense of mankind)."

But GOD forces men to do things, and then punishes
them for doing of the same (according to Thomas
Hobbes).

The odious conclusion that follows from these premisses, Hobbes endeavours to shake off by making an
equally odious exception to the major premiss. He
would have the proposition, 'He who forces another

to do a thing, and then punishes him for doing of the same, is unjust,' not to hold good when GOD is the subject. Let us hear his own words:

"The power of GOD alone without other helps is sufficient justification of any action He doth. That which men make amongst themselves here by parts and covenants, and call by the name of justice, and according whereunto men are accounted and termed rightly just or unjust, is not that by which GOD almighty's actions are to be measured or called just, no more than His counsels are to be measured by human wisdom. That which He does is made just by His doing it; just, I say, in Him, though not always just in us. . . Power irresistible justifies all actions, really and properly, in whomsoever it be found: less power does not, and because such power is in GOD only, He must needs be just in all actions. . . GOD cannot sin, because His doing a thing makes it just, and consequently no sin; as also because whatsoever can sin is subject to another's law, which GOD is not. And therefore it is blasphemy to say GOD can sin; but to say that GOD can so order the world, as a sin may be necessarily caused thereby in a man, I do not see how it is any dishonour to Him."

These words come well from the author of the *Leviathan*. In that work Hobbes maintains that justice does not belong to the nature of man otherwise than as a fruitless velleity; that in a world of mutual wrong-doing, where might is right, justice comes into being only by dint of a convention, which binds men to live in society, and employs the strength of society for the curbing of the natural predaceousness of indi-

2

viduals. But GOD, as He fears none, has no occasion
for any such convention: consequently justice, such as
obtains between man and man, has no analogue in the
Hobbesian Deity, who, superior to all compacts, knows
no justice but power, no right but might.

"It is worthy of remark that the doubt whether
words applied to GOD have their human signification
is only felt when the words relate to His moral attributes; it is never heard of in regard to His power. We
are never told that GOD's omnipotence must not be
supposed to mean an infinite degree of the power we
know in man and nature, and that perhaps it does not
mean that He is able to kill us, or consign us to eternal
flames. The divine power is always interpreted in a completely human signification." *

Words applied to GOD have not their mere human
signification, as Mill here supposes, nor have they
a signification quite unconnected with humanity, as
Hobbes thought; but their signification in regard to
GOD is analogous to their signification in regard to men.
Man is a finite model of the infinite GOD: so far as he
exists, he exists after the image of GOD: all his positive qualities reflect the Author of his being. As man
to GOD, so stand man's ways to GOD's ways: they are
not the same in kind, but the same in proportion,—
even as the being of the globe and the being of the
globe's roundness are not homogeneous but analogous
being. This view strikes a mean between the Epicurean
high and dry deism, instanced by Hobbes, and the
anthropomorphism into which Mill (*loc. cit.*) appears

* Mill's *Examination of Sir W. Hamilton's Philosophy*, chap. vii.

to fall. The issue is admirably arbitrated by St Thomas Aquinas. But to understand him, we need to understand the terms "univocal," "equivocal" and "analogous." Mill shall explain them to us:

"A name is 'univocal,' or applied univocally, with respect to all things of which it can be predicated *in the same sense;* it is 'equivocal,' or applied equivocally, as respects those things of which it is predicated in different senses. . . . An equivocal or ambiguous word is not one name, but two names, accidentally coinciding in sound; . . . one sound, appropriated to form two different words. An intermediate case is that of a name used 'analogically or metaphorically'; that is, a name which is predicated of two things, not univocally or exactly in the same signification, but in significations somewhat similar, and which being derived one from the other, one of them may be considered the primary and the other a secondary signification. As when we speak of a brilliant light and a brilliant achievement." *

Mill has explained "metaphorical analogy." There is also "analogy proper," which is the proportion that obtains between similar things of different grades of being. The analogy which St Thomas has to speak of is "analogy proper." † We are now prepared to give ear to St Thomas.

" Difference in manner of being is a bar to the univocal application of the name 'Being.' Now GOD's manner of being is different from that of any creature; for GOD is Being in His own right, a prerogative not attaching to any creature out of GOD. Hence being is by no means predicable univocally of

* *Logic,* bk i, chap. ii, § 8.
† See Berkeley's *Minute Philosopher*, iv, 20, 21.

GOD and the creature; neither is any other predicate applied univocally to both. But some have said that there is no predicating anything even analogically of GOD and the creature; the predication common to the two is, they say, merely equivocal. That opinion, however, cannot be true; for in the pure equivocal use of terms a name is given to one thing without reference to another thing to which it is also given; whereas whatsoever things are said of GOD and of creatures are said of GOD with some reference to creatures, or of creatures with some reference to GOD. Besides, since all our knowledge of GOD is gathered from creatures, if there shall be no agreement betwixt the two except in name, we can know nothing of GOD but empty names with no realities underlying them. Therefore, we must say that nothing is predicable univocally of GOD and of the creature; nor yet are their common predicates predicated purely equivocally; but they are predicated analogously with reference of one to the other, as being is predicated analogously of substance and of quantity."*

Man occupies a certain position relatively to his Creator, and other positions relatively to his fellowmen. What his Creator may do to him, that may he do to his fellows in an analogous case. If no analogous case can ever occur, then it is in vain our going about "to vindicate the ways of GOD to man." On that supposition we cannot even call GOD just, since He is not just with any proportion to a human standard. Were an officer to keep a soldier in enforced detention from parade, and then flog him for being away, the union of those two acts would argue injustice in the doer of them. Nor would the injustice be diminished, but rather

* *De Potentia Dei*, q. vii, art. 7.

increased, by the thing being done by the commander-in-chief, by the king, nay, by an absolute monarch of the universe. Analogously, if my almighty Creator "so" ordered the world as a sin might be necessarily caused in me, and then punished me for that sin; certainly such a Creator would forfeit in my regard His title of 'just.' *

"Power irresistible justifies all actions, really and properly." As properly might Hobbes have said the same of immensity or of eternity. The Eternal and Immense Almighty can do no wrong; but it is not His omnipotence, any more than His eternity or immensity, that justifies what He does. He is peculiarly One GOD; and to speak of Him becomingly, we should have a name to express His perfections all in one. But that holy and awful name cannot dwell on mortal lips. The title which He takes in Exodus iii, 13, 14, "I am who

---

* Hobbes *On Liberty and Necessity* must have been lying open before Mill, when he penned this celebrated outburst: "If, instead of the 'glad tidings' that there exists a being in whom all the excellences which the highest human mind can conceive exist in a degree inconceivable to us, I am informed that the world is ruled by a being whose attributes are infinite, but what they are we cannot learn, except that 'the highest human morality which we are capable of conceiving' does not sanction them; convince me of it, and I will bear my fate as I may. But when I am told that I must believe this, and at the same time call this being by the names which express and affirm the highest human morality, I say in plain terms that I will not. Whatever power such a being may have over me, there is one thing which he shall not do; he shall not compel me to worship him. I will call no being good, who is not what I mean when I apply that epithet to my fellow-creatures; and if such a being can sentence me to hell for not calling him so, to hell I will go " (Mill's *Examination of Sir W. Hamilton's Philosophy*, chap. vii). This vehement language may be pardoned for the badness of the theology which evoked it.

am," would yield to prayerful study perhaps our fullest attainable notion of what GOD is and can. But since our every conception of GOD is inadequate, we endeavour by many different conceptions to compensate for the inadequacy of each. Having realised as best we may what Supreme Being means, we next regard that Being as containing the fullness of all the perfections that are distinguishable in creatures: accordingly we call Him All-wise, All-good, going through the list of the divine attributes so far as we have had experience of copies of them in creation. Each of these attributes intimately involves the rest. None can be almighty who is not eternal, immense, and infinitely holy. Still the name of each attribute stands for that one attribute, not for the rest. By *All-wise* we do not mean *Eternal:* neither does *Almighty* mean *All-holy.* Therefore Hobbes did wrong to assert that GOD was holy by virtue of His omnipotence. True, GOD is infinite holiness, and GOD is infinite power: but we look at GOD in one way when we call Him holy, and in another way when we call Him almighty; which two ways being diverse and distinct, it is a falsehood in our mouths and with our conceptions to say that GOD is holy because His power is irresistible. What we mean by power does not constitute or involve what we mean by holiness.

VI

"The necessity of an action doth not make the laws that prohibit it unjust. . . No law can possibly be unjust, inasmuch as every man maketh, by his consent, the law he is bound to keep. . . What necessary cause soever precede an action, yet if the action be forbidden, he that doth it willingly may justly be punished. For instance, suppose the law on pain of death prohibit stealing, and that there be a man, who by the strength of temptation is necessitated to steal, and is thereupon put to death, does not this punishment deter others from theft? Is it not a cause that others steal not? Doth it not frame and make their wills to justice? To make the law is, therefore, to make a cause of justice, and to necessitate justice; and, consequently, it is no injustice to make such a law. The intention of the law is not to grieve the delinquent for that which is past and not to be undone, but to make him and others just that else would not be so, and respecteth not the evil act past, but the good to come. . . But you will say, how is it just to kill one man to amend another, if what were done were necessary? To this I answer, that men are justly killed, not for that their actions are not necessitated, but because they are noxious. . . We destroy, without being unjust, all that is noxious, both beasts and men."

This passage is marked by a lucidity and vigour truly admirable. It is a splendidly bold and a scientifically accurate presentment of the philosophy of determinist punishment. My objections to that philosophy I have set forth in *Political and Moral Essays*, in the essay on *Morality without Free Will*, particularly pp. 253-259. My objections come to this, that while there is abundant ground on utilitarian principles for visiting with pain the offender who has unfortunately been determined to the injury of society,—for the pain will readjust his determination,—there is nevertheless no ground for visiting him with any moral disapprobation: you may call him names, significant of moral reproach, as stimulants corrective of his will, but in your heart you cannot reproach him, for what else could he have done?

VII

"If there be a necessity that an action shall be done, or that any effect shall be brought to pass, it does not therefore follow that there is nothing necessarily requisite as a means to bring it to pass; and therefore, when it is determined that one thing shall be chosen before another, it is determined also for what cause it shall so be chosen, which cause, for the most part, is deliberation or consultation, and therefore consultation is not in vain."

Hobbes signifies that the necessity of an action is a conditional necessity, dependent upon a certain state of mind going before. Hence he notes the unreasonableness of withdrawing the condition and still looking for the action as a thing that must ensue. But the condition itself, he says, is supplied of necessity, following upon other antecedent conditions likewise necessary, and so up to some primitive collocation of circumstances, the parent egg, whence the phases of the universe, from yesterday to to-day, for ever, are perpetually proceeding according to a law of mathematical rigour. With this vast concatenation of conditional necessities the acts of our will interlink. The conditions which inexorably determine those acts pre-existed cycles untold before our birth. The primitive nebula bore within its bosom the seeds which were, of sure necessity, to develop into the doings of every agent that should populate the solar system, the shooting of meteors, the revolutions of planets, the spots on the sun, and the feelings, thoughts and volitions of men. Any bystander with an eye to see, and an intellect to comprehend, might have perused the universal history of the system, printed entire in that early primer. The thread of our lives was hackled and twisted ere our mothers conceived us. We rise too late in the parliament of the world to move any amendment. Our puny individualities may not stand between cause and effect. We are children, creatures of the arrangements that were before us: we are their slaves. Our function is to do their bidding and die. We exist in fulfilment of a destiny, whereof we hold in our hands neither the beginning, middle, nor end. Each man's lot in life is designed and constructed for him; none is his own architect in that matter: though the expiring eloquence of the Roman Chatham did protest to the contrary: *Faber quisque mortalium fortunæ suæ*. Fortune to us is, not as the web to the spider, spun out of ourselves, but rather as the web to the fly, catching us in its meshes. Only, with less initiative than the fly, we do not wing our own flight into the entanglement; we are born there. Fortune's web is very old, hanging from the pillars of creation and coeval with them. Fortune's web is very broad:

> A covering net, that nor sinner nor saint
> Can 'scape from the circle of slavish constraint
> And captive woe complete.*

Yes, and of captive joy, too; the house of feasting with the house of mourning is alike a house of bondage.

On such a system it is idle for any man to question with his own soul what he means to do. What he must

---

* Æschylus, *Agamemnon*, 346.

do is written even to the last detail. We need not use our own judgements: there is no seat for us at the council board where the march of our lives is planned. Circumstances may be relied upon to galvanise us, when the hour for action arrives. We shall be equal to the occasion, so far forth as the occasion shall raise us to its level. For if, as Hobbes confesses, the consultation, the necessary prelude to the action, is secured and cannot fail,—secured by a chain of antecedents reaching back to before the birth of the consultor,—that person infallibly will find himself consulting and acting, if necessity will have him so; even as some day he will find himself dying, without any labour of his, thanks to the sure, steady thud of necessity battering ceaselessly at the portal of animal life. Consultation, in this view, is not in vain; neither is digestion; but, to use a colloquial phrase, "it comes natural" to one to deliberate as to digest.

Denial of the freedom of the will does not involve a renunciation of that freedom in practice. A man cannot divest himself of a property so connatural. If GOD creates, we must be, and be of the specific nature that GOD specifies. The very neglect of freedom is an exercise of liberty in us: it is the part of a free man playing the slave. Fatalism abounds in the East.* Philosophers further westward have taught necessarian doctrines, rigid as ever Sultan acquiesced in. But their speculative fetters, a looser fit than the Grand Turk's, can be slipped off upon occasion, to permit of a scamper with free limbs after the butterflies of temporal profit. We

* Cf. Palgrave's *Arabia*, vol. I, pp. 365-368.

never witness the part of a necessarian played on 'Change, nor in the Houses of Parliament, nor in Westminster Hall. In the disabusing air of civil emulation our countrymen understand that success depends on the fight which men make to gain it; that fighting any fight, good or bad, comes, not of motives simply, but ultimately and mainly of a man's own will and deliberate espousal of motives.

Because in the affairs of this world necessarians exhibit as much self-determination as their opponents, the denial of free will passes for an error, if it be an error, of pure theory, void of evil consequences to pure morals. Unfortunately, morality follows from theory, and varies with theory, far more closely than business does. The ends of business stare us in the face,—money and manufactures, things of gross and palpable advantage. But the ends of morality glimmer in the distance like stars calm and cold and high overhead. If we are Christian just men, we live by faith, which is the evidence of things unseen. If, again, our justice be the justice of a heathen naturalism, still its mainsprings are abstract contemplations of the intellect, such as honour or the happiness of society, not objects of sense. The ends of business are attractive enough of themselves to rouse an Englishman to work with a will, necessarian though he be. Not so the ends of morality in the case of the multitude of mankind, once they get to believe that they cannot help doing whatever they do. It is somewhat of a risk to guarantee any mortal's remaining a moral man far into the future; but a peculiar instability vexes his moral position, who writes himself down a log brandished in necessity's arms. The suspicion that one is being tempted above one's strength must furnish a frightful lever to temptation. It is not a suspicion that a wise father would wish to awaken in his child. Yet, if the will is not free, the suspicion is too well-founded, all sins in that case being examples of men tempted above their strength.

Hobbes so trembled in prospect of the pernicious construction to which his opinion was liable, that he wrote: "It is true that ill use might be made of it, and therefore your Lordship [the Marquis of Newcastle] and my Lord Bishop [Bramhall of Londonderry] ought, at my request, to keep private what I say here of it. And in conclusion I beseech your Lordship to communicate it only to my Lord Bishop."

VIII

"For praise and dispraise they depend not at all on the necessity of the action praised or dispraised. For what is it else to praise, but to say a thing is good? Good, I say, for me, or for some one else, or for the State and commonwealth. And what is it to say an action is good, but to say it is as I wish? or as another would have it, or according to the will of the State? that is to say, according to the law. Does my Lord think that no action can please me or him or the commonwealth that should proceed from necessity? Things may therefore be necessary and yet praiseworthy, as also necessary and yet dispraised, and neither of them both in vain, because praise and dispraise and likewise reward and punishment do by example make and conform the will to good and evil."

To praise a thing is to pronounce it good in its kind.

A thing is praised for having the excellence proper to its nature. Praise implies approval. The statement therefore is not a correct one, that to praise is to affirm a thing to be as I would wish. I may wish a being for private ends of my own to have not the excellence that it ought to have. The burglar wishes the lock of the safe to be ill-made; he wishes the servant of the house to be unfaithful. If lock and servant do yield to his tampering, he is pleased, but finds it not in his heart to praise them. He despises them both, the one for a good-for-nothing manufacture, the other for a good-for-nothing man.

Inanimate things are praised for their beauty or usefulness. Products of art are praised inasmuch as they answer the end for which man made them. Plants and brute beasts are praised for their full and perfect growth or promise of growth, according to their species. And for what is man praised? Man is praised for exhibiting in himself what belongs to the perfection of human nature. He is praised for stature, strength and beauty, for quickness of understanding, for talent to command. He is praised to a large extent for what nature in a particular case and circumstances have made him. But the praise of man stops not there. When it has been said of an individual that he is tall and handsome and intelligent, what is most to his praise or dispraise remains still to be told. There is the question of conduct: whether he lives up to his nature as man behaving reasonably or whether he is the slave of passion, the sport of the solicitation of the hour. On his conduct it depends whether or no we shall call him a praiseworthy man.

A thing may be necessary and still praised. But the term 'praiseworthy' is reserved for those actions alone which are commonly taken to be not necessary, the actions of the human will in the sphere of merit or duty. Praise is an approval that may be bestowed on any being or agency; but praiseworthiness is a title to what is called 'moral approbation.' Praiseworthiness comes of acting up to the dictates of reason, to the counsels of generosity, to the requirements and capabilities of a moral nature. A moral nature has power within certain limits to make or mar itself. A brute nature is made or marred simply in accordance with primitive endowment and supervening circumstances. In other words a moral nature is free. It does not grow by a physical and necessary course towards the perfection that becomes it. It tends thither by self-determined acts in keeping with a law of command, not of inevitable effect. A morally good being, then, is to a certain extent the cause and author of his own goodness; not so the nature, however admirable for beauty or fertile of profit, that simply is what it is, and does what it does, because it is made so to be and so to act.

Hobbes insists on ignoring that special quality of praise which is bestowed on free agents, and is expressive of the sentiment of moral approbation. According to him we praise a hero and a hurricane just alike, when both have done the like work of discomfiting an enemy's Armada, except that we applaud the hero with a prudential regard to the future, hoping to move him or others to repeat the performance when the emergency shall recur. But does not this intention to stimulate by

praising come as an afterthought? Is not the first burst
an outpouring of pure admiration and commendation,
without respect to any recurring need. Is praise to be
included under the sarcastic definition of gratitude,
"a lively sense of future favours"? So it appears on
Hobbes's showing. But Hobbes's philosophy is one
continuous piece of sarcasm on humanity.

IX

"Piety consisteth only in two things: one, that we
honour GOD in our hearts, which is that we think as
highly of His power as we can . . . the other is that
we signify that honour and esteem by our words and
actions. . . He therefore that thinketh that all things
proceed from GOD's eternal will, and consequently are
necessary, does he not think GOD omnipotent? . . .
Again, he that thinketh so, is he not more apt by external acts and words to acknowledge it?"

Piety, called in Greek εὐσέβεια, "due reverence,"
in Latin, *pietas*, "filial duty," was defined by the Platonists "justice towards the gods"; by the Stoics, "the
science of serving the gods."* The notion of piety according to these definitions depends upon the notion
of GOD. GOD is to be reverenced as His dignity merits:
He must have that duty paid Him which His pater-
nity demands: He must have that justice done Him
to which His authority has a right: He must receive
service in that quality and in that degree in which He
is master. To people who know little about GOD, His
power is His most striking attribute; even as, placed
at a distance from a noble edifice, the chief feature we

* Trench's *New Testament Synonyms*, xlviii.

appreciate about it is size. After the power of GOD,
His justice becomes known; and so, after the appreciation of size, there follows, on a nearer view, the
appreciation of proportion. Not till we stand on the
threshold of the building, does our eye kindle to the
sight of its delicate carving and variegated splendours;
even so GOD must draw us very near to Himself ere
we can enter into and reciprocate His tenderness and
love. The tyro in piety is slavishly afraid of GOD: the
proficient in piety tempers this slavish fear with hope:
the expert in piety fears GOD with a filial fear, he hopes
in GOD, he does more,—he loves Him. The timid tyro
hardly looks upon GOD as a person: the sentiment of
fear is fully entertainable of things. The trustful proficient awaits the sentence to be passed upon him by
the person of his "just Judge." But to the loving expert GOD is a father; and the father is the first of persons in his child's eyes. There is no thorough piety
towards a GOD of mere power, nor even towards a
GOD of mere justice; the adequate object of piety is
a GOD of justice and power blended into love. But
Hobbes's Deity is not good: He is nothing more than
omnipotent. Else why should piety consist in this, that
we think as highly of His power as we can, to the exclusion of His goodness?

Opening the eleventh chapter of Isaias, which an-
nounces the coming of a GOD far other than him
whom necessarians imagine, we read: "And the spirit
of the LORD shall rest upon him, the spirit of wisdom
and understanding, the spirit of counsel and fortitude,
the spirit of knowledge and piety; and there shall fill

him the spirit of the fear of the LORD." From this passage the Church has drawn her enumeration of the seven gifts of the Holy Ghost. St Thomas Aquinas defines the phrase "gift of the Holy Ghost," and shows in what sense piety falls under the definition. "The gifts of the Holy Ghost," he says, "are certain habitual dispositions of the soul, whereby it is readily susceptible of the impulses of the Holy Spirit. Among other things, the Holy Spirit moves us to this, to cherish a filial affection towards GOD, according to the text (Rom. viii, 15), 'Ye have received the adoption of sons, whereby we cry, Abba, Father.' And since to piety it properly belongs to pay duty and reverence to a father, it follows that the piety whereby we pay duty and reverence to GOD is a gift of the Holy Ghost."* This piety of filial affection is the kind inculcated by St Peter: "Provide, in the exercise of your faith, virtue; and in your virtue, knowledge; and in your knowledge, self-restraint; and in your self-restraint, patient endurance; and in your patient endurance, piety; and in your piety, brotherly love; and in your brotherly love, charity."† On the clause, "in your patient endurance, piety," Dean Alford has the paraphrase: "Let it not be mere brute stoical endurance, but united with GOD-fearing and GOD-trusting."‡ He quotes another commentator's remark, that, in this company of virtues, we see "faith leading the band, love closing it." But brute stoical endurance, little better than that of the devils, who "believe and tremble,"§ is all the piety,

---

* 2a 2æ, q. cxxi.   † 2 Pet. i, 5, 6, 7.
‡ *New Testament for English Readers.*   § James ii, 19.

all the "justice towards God" rendered by Thomas Hobbes, all the "science of serving God" that a necessarian knows.

X

"For repentance, which is nothing else but a glad returning into the right way, after the grief of being out of the way; though the cause that made him go astray were necessary, yet there is no reason why he should not grieve; and again, though the cause why he returned into the way were necessary, there remained still the causes of joy. So that the necessity of the actions taketh away neither of those parts of repentance, grief for the error and joy for returning."

By a rule of logic, a definition should not be *latius definito*, wider than and including more things than the thing defined. Hobbes's definition of repentance as "a glad returning into the right way after the grief of being out of the way" sins against this rule. It would apply to the case of a traveller lost on a moor, and afterwards finding the track again, a glad recovery which none but Thomas Hobbes would exalt into repentance. Surely the tears of Mary Magdalen flowed from some other source.

There is nothing *moral* in Hobbes's philosophy.

XI

"Though prayer be none of the causes that move God's will, His will being unchangeable, yet since we find in God's word, He will not give His blessings but to those that ask, the motive of prayer is the same. Prayer is the gift of God no less than the blessing, and the prayer is decreed together in the same decree wherein the blessing is decreed. . . Prayer . . . though it precede the particular thing we ask, yet is not a cause or means of it, but a signification that we expect nothing but from God. . . . The end of prayer, as of thanksgiving, is not to move but to honour God Almighty, in acknowledging that what we ask can be effected by Him only."

Rather, the prayer is foreseen in the decree wherein the blessing is decreed. Thus God, foreseeing from eternity that certain creatures will pray for fine weather on a certain day, has passed His eternal *fiat* that that day shall be fine. The prayer is indeed the gift of God no less than the blessing. "Every good gift and every perfect gift is from above."* Prayer being a better and more perfect gift than sunshine, it would be absurd to pretend that we owed sunshine to God and not prayer. But our free will co-operates with the grace of prayer which God gives us; while the sun shines upon us *willy nilly*. Prayer is the better gift, precisely because, inviting our co-operation, it becomes more our own.

I may inquire why God will not give His blessings but to those that ask. I gather from Hobbes that it is because the Almighty wishes to receive from us the honour of an acknowledgement that the beneficial result which we desire can be effected by Him only. He wishes us to confess our thorough dependence on Him. That, I think, is truly the reason of the institution of prayer. But it supposes the confession on our part to be free. It is no honour to a lord to seize his vassal's hand and trace therewith, by stronger contraction of muscle, a signature to a declaration of allegiance. It

* James i, 17.

may be honourable to have persons under one in a state of constrained subjection; but there can be no access of honour from compelling them, without possibility of denial, to declare that they are in constraint. GOD has creatures who serve Him perforce,—the whole of irrational nature. But He does not expect confession from them. It is true that the Psalmist has, " Confess to the LORD, ye heavens "; * and, " The heavens are telling the glory of GOD."† These sayings mean that the heavens tell the glory of GOD to man, and incite him to confess to the LORD. Man is the high priest of the universe, gathering up the unconscious worship of the rest of creation to present it consciously to the Creator. Another verse is, " Let all thy works confess to thee, O LORD."‡ If all, then also Thy reprobate works, the devils and spirits of the damned. These confess of necessity and against their will. But there is reason for constraint in their case. GOD is wringing from them perforce that homage which they refused Him while they were free. He has bound them physically, for that they broke through moral bonds. They would not serve, and He has made them slave. Hobbes insists that the tribute exacted from hell is the type and model of whatsoever honour ascends to GOD from any of His creatures. I cannot but think such a doctrine an exceeding insult to the Most High.

XII

" The nature of sin consisteth in this, that the action done proceed from our will and be against the law. . . Now when I say that the action was necessary,

* Ps. cxxxv, 26.   † Ps. xviii, 1.   ‡ Ps. cxliv, 10.

I do not say that it was done against the will of the doer, but with his will, and necessarily."

The nature of sin consisteth in this, that the action done proceed from our will with advertence, and be against the known law. An action done from impulse, a hasty blow struck in passion, has an excuse from sin. So far as it was sinful, the agent knew what he was doing. Perhaps a series of sinful yieldings to impulse had formed in him a habit of yielding. That habit it was, of his own formation, which communicated to the passionate impulse the force which he did not withstand. He was to blame for the strength of an evil tendency which had been strengthened by himself. Impulsive action is less pardonable in an adult than in a child, who has not lived long enough to form habits whether of licence or self-restraint. Again, to be sinful, an action must be against a known law. Against a law unknown, which there was no ground to surmise and no obligation to ascertain, there can lie no sin. In cases where the law is imperfectly known, breach of law is excused to the extent of the transgressor's invincible ignorance. Hence a higher intelligence sins more guiltily than a lower one. The higher intelligence is both better conscious of its own act, and better appreciative of the sacred character of the obligation which it violates.

Hobbes speaks of action done with the will of the doer and necessarily. I am far from replying that this phrase involves a contradiction. An action may well be voluntary and necessary at the same time. Such may be some of our actions in this life, in early years especially. The act of loving GOD, in the saints who see

Him face to face, is voluntary and necessary. Whenever an object under advertence perfectly satisfies our longing, we will that object and we cannot but will it. If our understanding is mean, mean are our longings, and our will is necessitated to acquiesce in mean things. Exalt the understanding, and you amplify the desires and elevate the will to greater liberty. But no will is free in reference to all possible objects. There must be some point of satiety to the mind's cravings: free will reigns up to that point, and no further. To an infant a toy marks the point of satiety; to a seraph, GOD. The infant fain must love the toy; the seraph fain must love GOD. Adult man on earth occupies an intermediate position. The toy satisfies him not thoroughly, nor does any worldly thing afford him thorough satisfaction. Even GOD is at present an inadequate object to his desire, owing to his imperfect realisation of the goodness of GOD. Therefore man remains free to choose between good and evil of the moral order. In that crisis, what GOD expects of him is that he shall fix his thought and his affection on the excellence of the divine law, which reason indicates, and turn away his mind from the sensible advantages of breaking that law, and will not to taste those sweets. Thus is man on trial in this world.

But it would be no fair trial, if, when a man knew an action to be against the divine will, still do it he must, with full consent and without ability to refuse; if, in other words, a sinful pleasure, adverted to as sinful, gave complete and unmixed satisfaction to human nature, and left man nothing to desire, nothing else to do but to sin. In that case, either there is no sin, or the author of the sin is the author of the necessity by which it is committed.

Hobbes rejects the Apocrypha: I bring therefore the son of Sirach, not as an authority to condemn, but as a sage to warn him:

Say not, It is owing to the LORD I fell away: for what he hateth, thou shalt not do.

Say not, he led me astray: for he hath no use for a sinful man.

The LORD hateth all abomination, and it is not lovely to them that fear him.

He made man from the beginning, and turned him loose in the power of his own deliberation.

If thou choosest, thou wilt keep the commandments, and give proof of thy resolution.

He has set before thee fire and water: to whichever thou choosest thou wilt stretch forth thine hand.

Before men is life and death, and whichsoever one resolves upon shall be given to him.

For great is the wisdom of the LORD, strong in principality, and seeing all things.

And his eyes are upon them that fear him, and he shall take cognisance of every work of man.

And he did not command anyone to be impious, and gave not permission to anyone to sin.*

XIII

"A man is then only said to be compelled, when fear makes him willing . . . as when a man willingly throws his goods into the sea to save himself. . . Thus all men that do anything for love, or revenge, or lust, are free from compulsion, and yet their actions may be as necessary as those that are done by compulsion; for sometimes other passions work as forcibly as fear."

* Ecclus xv, 11-20, from the Greek.

Aristotle* examines the question whether a man who willingly throws his goods into the sea to save himself can be said to do so under compulsion. And he concludes that,—defining a compulsory act to be one "the origination of which is from without, the party compelled contributing nothing,"—such an act of jettison cannot be pronounced compulsory. What is compulsory is the owner's distress between two alternatives, the abandonment of his goods on the one side, and the likelihood of perishing with them on the other. There he stands, as we say, "between the devil and the deep sea." His liberty is circumscribed between two terms, neither of which he likes. Yet is he free to attach himself to either term, to choose either the certainty of a loss of fortune or the imminent risk of a loss of life. Loss or risk, one or other he must choose, but he will choose either of them freely. The jettison would be then compulsory, if the captain were to lock the merchant up in the cabin while his wares went by the board without his concurrence.

The Christians, whom the pagans threatened with death if they refused incense to Jove, furnish another case in point. They could not help having to choose between death and apostasy, but they could help on which side their choice lay. For that reason we honour the martyrs, while CHRIST has judged the guilt of them that denied Him. It would be improper to call their denial compulsory.

At the same time, acts of that kind, to which men consent rather than brave a threat, frequently go by

* *Nicomachean Ethics*, III, i.

the name of compulsory in common parlance. We say that a traveller was compelled to fee the brigand who clapped a pistol to his ear. I admit that there is this usage of speech. Neither do I deny that sometimes other passions work as forcibly as fear. I conceive a father, whose child has been murdered, being at least as strongly prompted to pursue the murderer for revenge as to fly from him for fear. Yet if he fled, he would be spoken of as having been compelled to retire; whereas there would be no mention of compulsion if he went in pursuit. That is true. Hobbes thence infers that a deed of vengeance is as much necessitated as a deed done by compulsion of fear. I may let pass the inference, for I deny that a deed done by compulsion of fear is necessitated. If my opponent, taking a loose phrase for a strict one, retorts that compulsion implies necessity, I straiten his lines and bring him back to the strictness of the Aristotelian definition: "An act is compulsory, the origination of which is from without, the party compelled contributing nothing." An act done from fear is not compulsory in that sense: for the frightened party contributes his own volition to remove himself from what he fears.

Yet there is ever some truth at the bottom of popular sayings about matters of morality. Not moral philosophers alone are moralists: all men are so. No trustworthy professor of moral philosophy will brand popular phrases on that subject as the mere expression of popular errors. Why then do the people in spite of Aristotle persist in calling those volitions compulsory which are elicited under intimidation? I hope I can show why.

In the first place I remark that a person, acting under
the spell of any passion whatsoever, is by no means
the free and authentic agent that he is when his act is
passionless. The more impassioned, the less free, at
the moment. For the freedom of the will is derived
through the intellect; it is the truth that makes us
free: but passion dazes the intellect and paints the
truth in false colours. The passion that infringes a
man's freedom may be the foster-child of his own
folly: then his past conduct is to blame for the strength
of temptation at the present hour. It is no excuse for
a guilty *amour* that the offender was over head and
ears in love: he plunged himself into the quagmire.
Forbidden love tempted, and he accepted by repeated
acts, till he converted a passing excitement into a chron-
ic disorder. There are some words of Aristotle that
go near to describing this case: "The sick man cannot with a wish be well again; yet . . . he is voluntarily
ill, because he has produced his sickness by living in-
temperately and disregarding his physicians. There
was a time then when he might have helped being ill;
but, now he has let himself go, he cannot any longer
recover himself; just as he who has let a stone out of
his hand cannot recall it, and yet it rested with him to
aim and throw it, because the origination was in his
power."*

But the passion of fear is unlike other passions.
Love, ambition, sloth are home-products; but fear
has rather the character of an importation. What a man
shall love rests pretty much with himself: what he shall

* *Nic. Eth.* III, vii, 14.

fear, not so much. Fearfulness is that key of our nature
on which our neighbour's fingers find it easiest to play
without our leave. I may make gifts to a man, and he
will not love me; do him wrong, and he will not hate
me; but let me threaten his life, and it will be very
hard if he does not fear me. Fear-prompted actions
then are less liable than the rest of impassioned actions
to be involved in the guilt of prior free acts that fostered the growth of the passion: for fear depends less
upon the free acts of the subject than do the other
passions. Free will has ordinarily more to say to anger
and love than to fear. This, I conceive, is the reason
why actions done under intimidation are popularly
palliated under the name of compulsory. But they are
not wholly excused by the people; nor are they proved
absolute necessities.

XIV

"One heat may be more intensive than another,
but not one liberty than another: he that can do what
he will hath all liberty possible, and he that cannot
hath none at all."

In a noun that is made to signify the mere attain-
ing or falling short of a certain measure, there is no
room for less and more. In an entrance examination
for a school, college or profession, some candidates
pass and some fail. All who pass gain entrance equally;
all who fail are equally excluded. We say, "more nearly
equal," or "more hopelessly lost"; but not "more
equal," "more dead," "more lost." Participles properly
so-called admit no comparative: nor do nouns substan-
tive that denote a species. Julius Cæsar was not more a

man than the meanest of the mean crew who murdered him; though he was more of a man perhaps than all of them together, and had stuff in him to furnish forth a dozen Brutuses.

Freedom, in Hobbes's definition, is ability to do as one likes. A fair specimen of this sort of freedom is found in that institution which Hobbes delighted to extol, the absolute monarch. One or other of three things: either the monarch alone of all the inhabitants of the realm is in any sense free; or the monarch is more free than his subjects; or monarch and subjects are equally free. The last proposition means that, under a despotic government, every man does as he likes. Probably that is what Hobbes would have said. He would have proceeded to explain, as in many of his writings,* how the will of the subject coincides with the will of the monarch by virtue of the compact whereby the people have made over their rights to one perpetual depositary. There is no use arguing the point. If anyone is pleased to say that a Russian goes to Siberia because he likes to go wherever the Tsar may send him, we can afford to let that whimsical thinker enjoy his own humour without contradiction. Nor need we stay to contend with any maintainer of the position that freedom of any kind, and consequently free will, is the exclusive prerogative of absolute monarchs, though that paradox might not unreasonably be built upon the Hobbesian saying that he who cannot do what he will hath no liberty at all. The remaining alternative is to allow that the will of an absolute monarch is more

* e.g., *De Civitate*, cap. xxi, De Libertate Civium.

free, by Hobbes's definition of freedom, than the wills of his subjects,—more free, because more powerful.

Nevertheless, free will is not to be confounded with the power to carry one's will into deed. A beggar's will may be as free as a king's. It may be more so. An act of the will is free, when the agent might have abstained from eliciting it, the circumstances relevant to the act remaining the same. A free act is not unconditioned, but it does not follow from the conditions as a matter of course. Now, if no more be here meant by freedom than the bare absence of necessity, and the mere fact that the agent could absolutely have done otherwise, it is clear that free will admits of no degrees, as neither does life: an animal must be either alive or dead. But there are degrees of fullness and intensity of life, and similarly of freedom. We do not say that he who can break prison by a great effort is as much at liberty as the man who can walk out by an open door. We commonly call that freedom greater which is more readily available and can be exercised more easily. At that rate, there are degrees in free will. An act is more free, then, in proportion as the agent could have done otherwise with greater facility. An act is more free the less it is conditioned. No free act, however, is wholly independent of conditions. So, to take an example, in the case of a strong propensity to drink, whether hereditary or self-acquired, if the propensity stops short of mania, the victim of it is not so entirely victim as wholly to cease to be a free agent, and yet, in common parlance, he is much less free than the well-bred and hitherto virtuous lady who is taking the first steps on the way of sipping.

Agents free and necessitated may be classified as follows in point of freedom and the reverse:

1. GOD.
2. Rational creatures, in final blessedness, having the sight of GOD.*
3. Rational creatures, still in the way of trial.
4. Irrational feeling creatures.
5. Insensible creatures.

Numbers 4 and 5 are necessitated in all their operations; number 3, in their chiefest operations, are free; numbers 1 and 2, in their chiefest operations, are necessitated. This may be briefly explained. An insensible thing, having no consciousness whatever, has no light to guide it to a choice; and, where there is no light, there is no liberty. A thing of this sort is not wholly passive, else it would be void of existence, but the active powers which it has are blind, and are led to their end by an external Being, the intelligent Creator of the insensible thing. A creature with senses, but without intellect and reason, has no reflex consciousness, no faculty of advertence to its own being and condition as such. Therefore, it acts always either on native impulse or by virtue of a training received from without. An agent like this is moved by springs of feeling, more or less complicated, which are not at its own command: it is not free. Rational creatures, on their trial in this world, have an intellect that informs them of unlimited good; they have a rational appetite that craves

* It is neither essential to my purpose, nor pleasantly accessory to it, to discuss the state of the will of rational creatures *in statu termini*, having no vision of GOD.

for unlimited satisfaction; they have a power of advertence to the spontaneous affection of their will, embra-
cing a satisfaction not unlimited and consequently not
adequate to their desire; they have then the liberty
either of continuing in the embrace of that satisfaction
or of desisting from it. Rational creatures, in final
blessedness, are endowed with the same boundless desire and the same advertence, but they have reached
their destination in the apprehension of a good, the recognised satisfaction of their immense desire: they are
not free to fall away from that Good, which is GOD
seen. Lastly, GOD Himself eternally beholds Himself,
eternally delights in Himself, eternally looks with com-
placence inward upon Himself as the worthy object of
His own satisfaction: GOD is not free not to love Himself.

The agents in class number 3, however, may sometimes be necessitated, while numbers 1 and 2 are upon
many points free. We often will without reflection: we
may occasionally encounter a satisfaction which fully,
or almost fully, meets our desire for the moment: our
volitions, thereupon, are not free or are hardly free.
Again GOD, and the blessed spirits who see His face,
find some good in created objects. The world is "very
good"; but, since GOD discerns in Himself an infinity
of better goodness, He was not necessitated to create
this world. The saints and angels have their favourites
on earth; yet, as none of us is good enough to enrap-
ture a seraph, we may be sure that, when the angels
love us, as Spenser says they do,* they love us freely.

* *Faerie Queene*, book II, canto viii.

Of freedom there is but one species, intelligent freedom: but we may distinguish intelligent necessity and brute necessity. A person lies under an *intelligent necessity* when, adverting to a complacency that fully satisfies his intellectual nature, he perseveres in that act of complacency. He cannot do otherwise than persevere: he knows better than to do otherwise than persevere. An agent that is fain to act without advertence lies under a brute necessity. This agent does things because it knows no better. An agent intelligently free, upon adverting to a complacency that does not fully satisfy his intellectual nature, may or may not persevere in the act of complacency. He knows of better things, but he may acquiesce to do that which now suggests itself as good.*

Numbers 4 and 5 (irrational creatures generally) lie wholly under the dominion of brute necessity, the ἀνάγκη of the Greek philosopher. Numbers 1 and 2 (GOD and the spirits which see His face) exemplify in the main an intelligent necessity of divine love, but they have also their freedom. Number 3 (rational creatures in the way of trial) rise in their best moments to the exercise of an intelligent freedom, whereby they merit reward or punishment. They walk in the border country between intelligent necessity and brute necessity. One or other of those realms shall be their home for eternity, according as they accomplish well or ill their transient course on earth.

It might, therefore, be expected, and experience

* It may be urged, But he does not know of better things to do under the circumstances. This difficulty will be faced in dealing with Locke.

proves the fact, that good men, yet in their flesh, approach to the state of angels, and bad men to the state of devils. I mean that the good, having GOD ever before their eyes, although in a glass, darkly, discern Him clearer and clearer by degrees, and proportionally diminish the possibility of their sinning; while the bad, who live away from GOD, grow more and more incapable of virtue. Thus good and bad alike abridge their freedom. True; but how do they abridge it? By exercising it.

This is how St Bernard speaks of the confirmed and hardened sinner: "That the soul, which could fall of itself, is unable further to rise of itself, proceeds from the will, which, enfeebled and prostrated by a spoilt and spoiling love of the corruptible body, is unequal to the undertaking of the love of justice. Thus, by a prodigy of strange perversity, the will, changed for the worse by sin, makes unto itself a necessity, in such a way that neither the necessity, being voluntary, can excuse the will, nor the will, being allured, can exclude the necessity. For this necessity is in a manner voluntary. It is a kind of courteous violence, overwhelmingly soothing and soothingly overwhelming; of which the guilty will, having once consented to sin, can neither shake itself free by its own sole effort, nor anywise excuse itself by reason."* This is a very sad necessity, as sad as the contrary necessity is happy. Between the

* *In Cantica,* sermo lxxxi. Cf. St Thomas, *Contra Gentiles,* b. iii, ch. clxi. The necessity here described is not physical, but moral: it implies, not utter impossibility, but enormous difficulty, which may, however, be surmounted by the grace of GOD. This is what the Saint means by saying that the fallen soul cannot rise of itself.

4

two we are striking out our course, away from this, towards that. The strokes that advance us are our own free acts. However, strike and act as we may, we are not to reckon on reaching any sure establishment in well-doing short of the grave. Nor, unless we choose to be very wicked, shall we achieve anything at all like confirmation in sin. The sea of freedom flows wide between these two opposite coasts. But the bottom shelves towards one and the other. The righteous in this world are drawing near to tread the firm earth of paradise, the land of immutable intelligent good; and the unrighteous are drifting on to the shore of that land of darkness and misery, where no order, but brute necessity of evil reigns.

XV

"The will follows the last opinion or judgement immediately preceding the action, concerning whether it be good to do it not. . . In that sense, the last dictate of the understanding does necessitate the action, though not as the whole cause, yet as the last cause, as the last feather necessitates the breaking of a horse's back."

The last opinion or judgement immediately preceding the action, concerning whether it be good to do it or not, is technically termed, "the last practical judgement." It is an old dispute in the schools, whether or no volition be determined by the last practical judgement; concerning which controversy three positions may be taken, none of them satisfactory:

1. Either the last practical judgement, which is supposed to determine the volition, is itself determined by

something else going before, so that we get an unbroken chain of necessary sequences,—and this is Hobbes's view here expressed; or the practical judgement, which determines the subsequent volition, is itself a free act; thus the will is free, not immediately in itself, but mediately, through the judgement on which it is necessarily conditioned; so that, instead of "free will," it would be more appropriate to speak of "free judgement," freedom being the immediate attribute, not of the will, but of the understanding.

2. Every judgement, in other than self-evident matter, involves a volition: you must "make up your mind" to judge, which means that your will must bring your understanding to act. Such a judgement, in scholastic phrase, is *elicited* by intellect, but *commanded* by will. Then, if every volition is determined by the last practical judgement, we have a *regressus in infinitum*, that same practical judgement being (usually) itself ruled by a volition. I say 'usually': where it is not so, the judgement is necessitated by the irrefragable evidence of the matter.

3. If, to escape these difficulties, you identify the last practical judgement with the volition to do the thing under deliberation, then the practical judgement determines itself; and the judgement being an act of intellect, the volition wherewith it is identified is an act of intellect also: where then remains the difference between intellect and will?

These three positions, with the perplexities which they involve, are all abolished by a distinction between a *spontaneous* practical judgement, which is the form which every practical judgement assumes to begin with, and a practical judgement *ratified and accepted by the will*, that is, a *voluntary* practical judgement, to which form not all practical judgements arrive. Upon this distinction I reply, in Thomist style, *ad 1ᵐ*, *ad 2ᵐ*, *ad 3ᵐ*.

Ad 1ᵐ. The practical judgement in its *spontaneous* stage does not determine the ensuing volition, except in a qualified sense presently to be explained. The *voluntary* practical judgement assumes its voluntary character consequently upon a volition, which, therefore, it does not determine. As an intellectual activity, the *voluntary* practical judgement is the matter of a free act, a thing freely *commanded*.

Ad 2ᵐ. Not every judgement is determined by a volition. As the argument allows, judgement in self-evident matter is not so determined. *Self-evident* means *evident upon full inspection*. But other matters, which are not evident when fully inspected, still present a *prima facie* appearance, sufficient to determine a *spontaneous* judgement, or what we call "an impression at first blush of the thing." This spontaneous judgement is not *commanded* by will, nor does it necessitate any subsequent volition, but it is matter for volition to go upon. The *regressus* could be urged against him only who was foolish enough to say that every volition is determined by a previous *voluntary* practical judgement.

Ad 3ᵐ. The *spontaneous* practical judgement clearly is not the volition to act accordingly, as such judgement is antecedent to all volition. When the resolve to act is taken, that *spontaneous* judgement is raised to the rank of a *voluntary* judgement. As it is in the intellect, however, it remains the matter of a volition; it is not the volition itself.

My own view is as follows. Every practical judgement begins in a form in which it is spontaneous and necessary. This spontaneous form is "valid," as canonists would say, i.e., it is a real judgement, but it is not "firm," i.e., it is liable to fail in securing approval from the will upon advertence, and so to pass away unauthorised and ineffectual. Yet if the will approve any practical judgement, it can for the nonce approve none other than the spontaneous judgement that is in possession, though it need not approve that: this measure of determinism is to be admitted. The last spontaneous practical judgement thus determines the will in this sense, that the will for the time being cannot go counter to that judgement in whatever it sanctions, as the traveller for the time being cannot take any train but that which is at the platform. And as the traveller always travels by the last train that draws up at the platform, by getting in and moving off and so seeing no more trains arrive; so the assent of the will, converting the spontaneous into the voluntary practical judgement, is always in accordance with the last practical judgement: for the adoption of one definite course of conduct leaves no room for approval of any other course.

XVI

" As soon as I can conceive eternity to be an indivisible point, or anything but an everlasting succession, I will renounce all that I have written on this subject [i.e., about the best way to reconcile contingence and liberty with the prescience and the decrees of God]. I know St Thomas Aquinas calls eternity, *nunc stans*, an ever-abiding now; which is easy enough to say, but though I fain would, yet I could never conceive it; they that can are more happy than I."

Any who share Hobbes's difficulty in conceiving the *nunc stans* may be referred to the eleventh book of St Augustine's *Confessions*. I here advance two propositions, countenanced by the Saint. First, that eternity is not an everlasting succession; and, secondly, that the very fact of succession evidences an everlasting *now*.

A succession is a series of changes. GOD does not change. Yet He is eternal. GOD's eternity therefore is not an everlasting succession.

There is an inverse relation between concentration of mind and sense of succession. The more the attention is fixed, the less advertence is given to the lapse of time, and *vice versa*. There is a well-known legend of a monk who chancing in the forest to light upon a bird, the song of which marvellously won his ear, stopped out all day, as he imagined, listening to the angelic songster,—for such it was,—and in the evening, returning to his monastery, found himself the lone remainder of a bygone generation, other men having reckoned a century what he counted one day. This, perhaps, is rather a tale of what would be than of what was. But, legend apart, who has not proved the unnoticed flight of hours over an interesting occupation? The mathematician, the poet, the saint lose all count of time; he in his calculation, he in his reverie, he in his prayer. But for the keen demands of appetite we might get becalmed for years, thinking of a favourite hobby, and awake, like Rip Van Winkle, from his protracted sleep, wondering how old we were. On the other hand, that day seems very long into which a variety of incidents has been crowded. Schoolboys sometimes remark what a length to look back upon their holidays appear, and that when they have enjoyed them keenly. The reason is, that holidays are a series of alternations of circumstances in striking contrast with the monotony of school-life. Each day of the vacation paints itself on new canvas: at school to-day does but deepen the picture of yesterday. The story of holidays is written out fair from leaf to leaf in an album. The story of school-days descends to memory on a palimpsest. When we say that a sailor has seen more life than a recluse of the same age, we mean that the sailor has felt more changes. In pain the tread of time is exceeding slow. This at first sight appears at variance with my theory. The sufferer apparently is confined to one thought, his pain. But I reply that the one thought of a creature in pain is pregnant with many thoughts. He seeks relief this way and that, and has no rest in his search. New trial and new failure, the one incessantly giving place to the other, make up the wriggling thing, the worm that never dies while the pain endures.* In pleasure also hours may seem long, but only in pleasure of the exciting kind, which makes the heart flutter and the thoughts fly wild. That is the pleasure of astonishment and expectation, rather than of fruition and content. There is a deeper and calmer

---

* The Greek word for anxiety, μερίμνα, was derived by the old etymologists from μερίζω, I divide, because, as Terence says, *curæ animum diversum trahunt.*

happiness where the heart is at rest. Of that type will be the eternal bliss of the saints. Face to face with the Object of their beatitude, and absorbed in the contemplation of the same, they will take even less note of time than the hermit in the legend: the everlasting years will roll on, measured by the motion of matter; but the thought, life and existence of the elect will remain a point, a *nunc stans*, an ever-abiding *now*, in the vision of GOD.*

To the same purpose St Augustine writes: "It has seemed to me that time is nothing but a lengthening out of what I know not; but I should be surprised if

---

*The relativity of time to the thinking mind is brought out in the following extract from Newman's *Dream of Gerontius*. The soul just departed wonders at not being immediately confronted with its Judge. The Guardian Angel accounts for the delay:

> For spirits and men by different standards mete
> The less and greater in the flow of time.
> By sun and moon, primeval ordinances,—
> By stars which rise and set harmoniously,—
> By the recurring seasons and the swing,
> This way and that, of the suspended rod,
> Precise and punctual, men divide their hours,
> Equal, continuous, for their common use.
> Not so with us in th' immaterial world;
> But intervals in their succession
> Are measured by the living thought alone,
> And grow or wane with its intensity.
> And time is not a common property;
> But what is long is short, and swift is slow,
> And near is distant, as received and grasped
> By this mind and by that; and every one
> Is standard of his own chronology;
> And memory lacks its natural resting points
> Of years and centuries and periods.
> It is thy very energy of thought
> Which keeps thee from thy GOD.

it were not a lengthening out of the mind itself."* "In thee, my mind, I measure periods of time. . . In thee, I say, the impression which passing things make upon thee endures even after they are past. What I measure is that present impression, not the things which have passed to cause it. That is what I measure when I measure periods of time. Therefore the periods of time are either that or nothing."† The holy doctor remarks that the mind fixed on GOD is "not distended but intent."‡ The mind in that case is not in time, if time is "a distension of the mind."

If the spirits who contemplate GOD are unmindful of succession, because they experience no change, much more will GOD Himself be changeless and without succession in His knowledge. Immutability enters into the essential concept of Deity. GOD is a self-existent Being. The self-existent cannot be material: matter without mind to support it is, in these days, a demonstrated absurdity. The Deity, therefore, is intelligent. And if intelligent, He knows Himself. Likewise He is the fountain of all possible existence. For possible existences are possible contingences, and the contingent must originate from the necessary, that is, from the self-existent, which is GOD alone. Were there two self-existents, there would be two orders of possibility, two regions of intellect, two truths. Since GOD is the intelligent origin of whatever can exist, He knows Himself and all things actual and possible in Himself. His knowledge, being thus infinite, must be unchanging: a change would be the introduction of a limit. GOD's

* *Conf.* xi, c. xxvi.   † *Ibid.* c. xxvii.   ‡ c. xxix.

mind, therefore, never changes. But, as we saw before, to a mind without change there is no time. Therefore there is no time to GOD. Yet GOD is eternal, as Hobbes confesses. Therefore the eternity of GOD is not an everlasting succession.*

Nay, succession would be impossible without some being that was not successive. Let us consider a human being running his course year by year. He is always growing older: he is always the same person: nay, he could not

* "*Is* alone in correct parlance belongs to the eternal Essence: *was* and *shall be* are expressions proper for creation that passes in time: for past and future are two states of transition, while that which is ever unswervingly the selfsame is like to become neither older nor younger by time, nor ever to have been created, nor to be now a creature, nor destined to be hereafter; and in a word it stoops not to undergo any of the alterations which creation has attached to the things that fleet before sense."—Plato, *Timæus* 38a.

"In the beginning, O LORD, thou hast laid the foundations of the earth, and the works of thine hands are the heavens: they shall perish, but thou remainest, and they all shall grow old like a garment: and as a vesture shalt thou change them, and they shall be changed; but thou, O LORD, art the selfsame, and thy years shall not fail."—Ps. ci, 25-27.

"Brethren, do not our years daily fail, and stand not still at all? For past years are not now, and future years are not yet. Now the former have failed, and the latter, that are coming, are coming to fail. In this one day then, brethren, lo, our present speech is in an instant. The hours gone by are past, the hours to come are not yet come; and when they are come, they too will pass and fail. What are the years that do not fail, but those that stand still? If, then, there the years stand still, the said years that stand still are one year, and the said one year that stands still is one day: which said one day has neither sunrise nor sunset, nor begins from yesterday, nor is cut off from to-morrow, but it stands always still, that one day. And you call that day what you will. If you will, it is years: if you will, it is a day. Whatever you think it, all the same, it stands still."—St Augustine on Ps. cxxi.

grow older if he did not remain the same person.* And he could not remain the same person, were there not a GOD, ever in every respect maintaining him in his personal identity. Succession implies permanence, variables imply a constant. Laying our hands on a friend's shoulder we say, 'This is he.' But this is he only for this instant: it is an inadequate view of him: in his full amplitude he is a being of many past instants linked on to endless futurities. The man is the subject of all his biography. Such is the meaning of personal identity. Though the man changes, it is always he who changes: the entire sum of changes are the changes of one person. There is an unchangeable element in man, by virtue of which he continues the same man. I am not arguing with the atheist: I suppose the reason of man's existence from moment to moment to be because GOD causes and wills that existence continually. Now a constant effect,—and man in his person and spiritual subsistency is a constant effect,—can be ascribed only to a cause that does not change. Changeable causes by their continued action produce changeable effects. If GOD were changeable, there would be nothing unchangeable in man, or anywhere in nature. Man would be a different person day by day: or rather there would be no personality in man at all, nor any substantial being in creation. As in man there is permanence under succession, so in GOD there is permanence without succession.

The Oriental emblem of eternity was a serpent with

* The impossibility of saying that anything changes if absolutely everything is always changing,—in other words, the impossibility of any Becoming (γένεσις) if there be no Being (οὐσία) anywhere,— is well argued by Plato, *Theætetus*, 181c-183b.

its tail in its mouth, forming a circle. Instead of a circle for the emblem I would propose a sphere, of radius infinite. At the centre of the sphere is GOD, seeing in Himself with one look the whole compass of possible creations, represented by great circles traceable on the sphere. A few great circles, actually traced there by His hand, represent actual creatures. GOD sees the whole circle round at once, not however as a point, but as a circle. And this illustration meets an objection, which has been put as follows: "A man has not the qualities which he had some years ago, but other qualities; he had not then the qualities he has now. If any one sees all these qualities existing together, which are not together, he does not see them more correctly, but less correctly."* GOD does not see qualities existing together which are not together, but He sees together the entire succession of qualities coming one after another. I refer the writer to his own remark, a few pages later: "Nothing is *completely* itself now, nor in a limited time: it needs everlasting time for that; for every monad is a focus of infinity."† The "now" he speaks of is the now of the creature, and in that sense the remark is just: but in the standing "now" of the Creator, in GOD's eternal vision, everything completely is. GOD does not progress with the world's progress, He is ever beforehand with it. The vicissitudes of the creature cast no shadow on Him who is the pure light of perfect Knowledge burning from the fullness of Being.

There are philosophers who deny all permanent exis-

---

* The Hon. Roden Noel in *Contemporary Review* for June, 1872, p. 94.　　　　　　　† Ibid. p. 99.

tence, inclusive of that which I call personal identity. They agree with Heraclitus that the universe is mere γένεσις, or becoming, without any subtratum of οὐσία, or being.* They say that I am conscious of mind in myself as a series of my own states of consciousness; that I think of other minds only in terms derived from my own; that mind, therefore, means to me a series of conscious states. This argues the impossibility of my conceiving any originating mind as first cause of the universe. "How is it possible for me to conceive an originating mind which I must represent to myself as a single series of states of consciousness, working the

* "The principal feature in the conception of being is rest, fixedness. Now the opposite of this is the principal feature in the conception of becoming. It is unrest, unfixedness. A thing never rests at all in any of the changing states into which it is thrown. It is in the state and out of it in a shorter time than any calculus can measure. In fact the universe and all that it contains are undergoing a continuous change in which there is no pause; and therefore since pause or rest is necessary to the conception of being, the universe cannot be said to be in a state of being or fixedness, but in a continually fluxional condition, to be a process, a becoming, that is, something always changing, and no one of its changes enduring or stopping during any appreciable interval of time. If the change could be arrested for a single instant, that would yield a moment of what might properly be called being; but inasmuch as no change can be so arrested, the universe is a continual creation, a continually varying process, a becoming"—Ferrier's *Lectures on Greek Philosophy*, Heraclitus, §10. Thus, as the professor goes on to exemplify, the velocity of a falling body is "always becoming," for it is "always changing." It has no "certain constant velocity for the smallest conceivable time." In the "roseate hues" of a "gorgeous sunset," "before any one colour has had time to be that colour, it has melted into another colour"; and "you never, even for the shortest time that can be named or conceived, see any abiding colour, any colour which really is." According to Heraclitus there is no more permanence about substances and persons than about the rate of a falling stone or the tints of a sunset; all things are in a flux and nothing endures.

infinitely multiplied sets of changes simultaneously going on in worlds too numerous to count, dispersed through a space that baffles imagination?"* How indeed, if really I be myself nothing but a flux of states of consciousness?

But it is not only God, His eternity and existence, that vanish under the analysis of Heraclitus; we and the objects of our experience equally disappear. We are always becoming older. But if nothing is permanent in us, it is not we that become older: the term *we* is inept. We do not become anything, and, according to Heraclitus, we are not anything. There is an end of us; an end also of what we experience, for nothingness can experience nothing. So one might improve upon the Heraclitean formula, and instead of "all things are in a flux" (πάντα ῥεῖ) read "all things have vanished" (πάντα ἔρρει), or with Napoleon flying from Waterloo, *Tout est perdu.*

Such is the evil end to which a philosophy comes which has made a bad start. The starting point of philosophy, and indeed of thought, is the fact of consciousness, *I am.* Thence our thought flies to beings distinct from ourselves, and to a being of beings, which is God, Speculative thinkers have dwelt upon the notion of being to the undue neglect of the I who am. They have ignored their own personality, and the personality of their Creator, to glorify an abstraction. Then the abstraction has been discovered to be an abstraction, and flung aside accordingly, without concern for its founda-

*Herbert Spencer in *Contemporary Review* for June, 1872, p. 151. A series of states of consciousness could not work the universe; but such a series is not God. See St Thomas, *Summa contra Gentiles,* 1, ch. liv.

tion in fact. Being has yielded to becoming. But the forgotten *ego* cries out against the usurpation both of being and becoming. Heracliteans are ever talking about themselves, and thereby giving the lie to their own impersonal teachings. When will these philosophers retrace their steps and start afresh from the practice of the Delphic counsel, "Know thyself"? Man's self is a noble object to study for its own sake; yet not for that sake would the counsel be worthy to be inscribed on a temple. An inscription fit for a holy place should contain a revelation of GOD. "Know thyself" contains that revelation: it induces knowledge of GOD. Psychology forms the groundwork of natural theology.

XVII

"Liberty is the absence of all the impediments to action that are not contained in the nature and intrinsical quality of the agent; as, for example, the water is said to descend freely, or to have liberty to descend by the channel of the river, because there is no impediment that way, but not across, because the banks are impediments. And though the water cannot ascend, yet men never say it wants the liberty to ascend, but the faculty or power, because the impediment is in the nature of the water and intrinsical. So also we say, he that is tied wants the liberty to go, because the impediment is not in him, but in his bands; whereas we say not so of him that is sick or lame, because the impediment is in himself."

Free will goes further than this. "The nature and intrinsical quality of the agent" determines his spontaneous attitude to any motive that is applied to him: it does not determine him to identify himself with that motive upon advertence, and make it his own by consent and acceptance. He so consents, if he does consent, that under the same collocation of motives, with the same character and antecedents, and under the same spontaneously determined attitude of will, he might still have held back his consent and not made up his mind to anything. The alternative for the moment, I observe once more, is not between consent and positive rejection: that would be "liberty of contrariety," and free will does not go so far. The alternative is between consent and the mere negative attitude of a mind not yet made up; between volition x and zero of volition: that is properly called "liberty of contradiction," and in "liberty of contradiction" human free will essentially consists. Evidently, this is more than "liberty from constraint," which is the utmost liberty that Hobbes and other determinists concede. Some of them are pleased to call it "self-determination," but their "self-determination" is not free will. These "self-determinists" are as good determinists, and as true necessarians, as Thomas Hobbes himself, only less outspoken.

Metaphorically, we say that the water flows *freely* in a river when it appears to flow according to its own choice, seeking its level as man seeks his good. We say that an untethered mare is *free* to run away, because she is left to her own proclivities. In a word, we call all those things *free* which are allowed to behave according to their natures. What then? Does it follow that a London citizen is not free in any higher sense than that in which a horse at grass, or the water of the Thames, is free? Hardly, unless it appear that the water and the horse are man's natural equals. But if humanity rises superior over bestiality and water-power, it may be expected that the citizen, following his nature, shall be free in one way; and Bucephalus and the Thames, following their respective natures, shall be free in their own way, but not in his. According to Hobbes, they are all free in the same way. He sapiently explains how the river is free, and concludes that man can have no other freedom.

Man's nature is neither purely material, nor purely animal, nor purely intellectual, but a compound of the three. A material nature moves whither it is drawn or thrust without feeling the motion, particle supplanting particle by mere material laws: an animal nature makes for pleasurable feelings and avoids painful feelings, real or imaginary; it is ruled by those feelings as a needle by a magnet. Various functions of man's organic life are discharged by animal appliances, when higher directive powers are in abeyance. An intellectual nature essentially knows itself. It is ruled by perfect good, according to the highest conception which it has framed of good. When man reflects what he is about, he occupies an intellectual position. Finding himself realising what is to him a thoroughly adequate and satisfactory good, he must will that object. But finding a good inadequate and unsatisfactory, he may hold back his volition. It is not in any nature to be ruled by what fails to content it. The swine devours its acorns perforce, for it has no sense of better things, and the acorns yield perforce to be crunched by the swine, for they have no sense at all. But man takes his food freely: he

5

has visions of what he prefers to meat and drink. An
anomaly here appears to obtain that, while brute matter
and brute beasts are guided in their behaviour by adequate objects, man alone is left to act upon inadequate
grounds. But we must remember that man, too, has
his adequate Object,—only out of reach for the present
life.

XVIII

"I conceive that nothing taketh beginning from
itself, but from the action of some other immediate
agent without itself; and that therefore, when first a
man hath an appetite or will to something, to which
immediately before he had no appetite nor will, the
cause of his will is not the will itself, but something
else not in his own disposing."

The meaning here is that all change is produced,
not by the subject of the change, but by some being
external to the subject. The assertion is true, and borne
out by enumeration of instances. Thus an element of
matter is moved, not by any self-moving agency,—for
it is inert,—but by the agency of another element. And
man's mind, it seems to me, never directly induces
upon itself a modification entirely new. I agree that,
"when first a man hath an appetite or will to something, to which immediately before he had no appetite
nor will, the cause of his will [in that first stage of
volition] is not the will itself, but something else not
in his own disposing." What I have denominated
"spontaneous complacency," results in the mind without the person's authorship: it arises either through a
sensation, as when one catches sight of a beautiful object; or through an association, as when the pre-

established connexion of thoughts brings up the idea of the destruction of an enemy. Such a complacency in me is not mine: I have neither summoned nor sanctioned it, although I may be to some extent responsible for its coming, inasmuch as my previous acts, or my present negligence, may have facilitated its access to me. I can exercise no act properly my own, no act, that is to say, of free will, without an antecedent act which is not properly my own, namely, an act of spontaneous complacency. For a free volition is a sustaining of a complacency spontaneously arisen, after advertence to the insufficiency of the same. And this distinction, between the spontaneous and the reflex act of the will, annuls Hobbes's conclusion here drawn, "that voluntary actions have all of them necessary causes"; for spontaneous volitions are traceable to necessary causes, but reflex volitions ordinarily are not.

XIX

"I hold that to be a sufficient cause, to which nothing is wanting that is needful to the producing of the effect. The same also is a necessary cause. For if it be possible that a sufficient cause shall not bring forth the effect, then there wanteth somewhat which was needful to the producing of it, and so the cause was not sufficient... That ordinary definition of a free agent, namely, that a free agent is that which, when all things are present which are needful to produce the effect, can nevertheless not produce it, implies a contradiction that is nonsense; being as much as to say the cause may be sufficient, that is to say necessary, and yet the effect shall not follow... That there is no such thing as an agent, which when all things requisite to action are present, can nevertheless forbear to produce it; or, which is all one, that there is no such thing as freedom from necessity, is easily inferred from that which hath been before alleged. For if it be an agent, it can work; and if it work, there is nothing wanting of what is requisite to produce the action, and consequently the cause of the action is sufficient; and if sufficient, then also necessary, as hath been proved before."

Wherever there is a cause sufficient, in the Hobbesian sense of the term *sufficient*, for a necessary effect, there the cause is necessary and the effect will necessarily ensue. All effects of matter acting upon matter are necessary effects. Wherever then material substances are found in collocation, there is necessarily wrought a determination towards movement, the effect of the action of matter on matter. But given a cause insufficient for a necessary effect, not even Hobbes would say that that cause was necessary, or that the effect was necessarily to follow. Now, in the human mind, a motion of complacency may possibly arise, which, being adverted to, will be necessarily sustained. That is the case where the object appears to the subject in the light of a perfect good. There we see a necessary volition complete. But suppose the object of the complacency, when examined, appears to be not without its drawbacks. Such an object is not a sufficient cause of a necessary volition. Man's will is above being necessitated by what does not satisfy his desire. Consequently no necessary volition will follow the apprehension of that object. If a volition does follow, it will be not necessitated but free. There is sufficient cause for a free volition, but not sufficient cause for a necessary volition.

At that rate, Hobbes would contend, no volition could follow at all. I am unable to agree with him there. The object of man's will is good. Perfect good he must love; imperfect good he may love. His necessary adhesion to the former does not cut him off from freely adhering to the latter. It is natural for him to love good in any shape, although not with a necessary love, except the good which he apprehends to be perfect. Let us contemplate the case of a mother with her child. Supremely dear he is to her heart. For his sake she loves what is connected with him,—his playmates, his playthings, clothes, pictures and familiar haunts,—all that is like him, and all that he is fond of. I have little doubt that her love for her son is necessitated. She cannot choose but love him. She cannot possibly will to do him an injury. But the things which she loves for his sake she regards with an inferior affection. She might find it in her heart to burn his likeness, though she could not allow the sun's rays to beat fierce on his head. The necessity under which she lies of loving him leads to a secondary love for what relates to him, which secondary affection, however, does not possess the cogency wherewith the primary love is endowed.

We must not forget that a free volition is not an entirely new move in the mind. Some motion towards the thing willed there was already, and that of necessity: the conscious acceptance and confirmation of that motion transforms it from necessary to free. Now I maintain as a notorious fact of consciousness, upon which no necessarian has ever thrown a doubt, that we are able advertently to make up our minds to an arrangement wherewith we are not altogether pleased. We subscribe our *Le Roi le veut*, though intelligence, the the king within us, conceives, and desire yearns after, a better measure than that. We then will without a sufficient cause for a necessary volition. *There wanteth somewhat which was needful to the production of it.* Therefore no necessary volition is produced; but the volition, which is produced, is free.

XX

"It is necessary that to-morrow it shall rain or not rain. If therefore it be not necessary it shall rain, it is necessary it shall not rain, otherwise there is no necessity that the proposition, it shall rain or not rain, should be true. I know there be some that say, it may necessarily be true that one of the two shall come to pass, but not singly, that it shall rain, or that it shall not rain, which is as much as to say, one of them is necessary, yet neither of them is necessary; and therefore to seem to avoid that absurdity, they make a distinction, that neither of them is true *determinate*, but *indeterminate;* which distinction either signifies no more but this, one of them is true, but we know not which, and so the necessity remains, though we know it not; or if the meaning of the distinction be not that, it hath no meaning, and they might as well have said, one of them is true *tityrice*, but neither of them *tupatulice.*"*

The handling this argument is simply an exercise in formal logic. If we consider what manner of asser-

---

* Tityre, tu patuli recubans sub tegmine fagi.—*Virgil*, Eclogue I.

tion a disjunctive proposition makes, we shall easily perceive that no proof of necessarianism can be extracted out of the law of excluded middle,—that everything necessarily either is or is not. Since the operations of inanimate nature, so far as that nature is concerned, are acknowledged on all hands to be necessary, I will alter the example to this: "It is necessary that to-morrow Philip shall sin or not sin." If Hobbes can show that sin in Philip, supposed to be alive and in the exercise of his faculties to-morrow, is either a necessity or an impossibility, he has gained the cause.

Logically examined, the disjunctive proposition, "To-morrow Philip must either sin or not sin," is tantamount to these two: (1) the assertion of Philip's sinning to-morrow necessarily involves the denial of his not sinning; (2) the denial of Philip's not sinning to-morrow necessarily involves the assertion of his sinning.

If Hobbes, out of these two propositions, can gather the conclusion that "if it be not necessary Philip shall sin, it is necessary he shall not sin," he is welcome to his victory. But he does not gather that conclusion out of those two propositions, but out of the two following, into which he virtually analyses the disjunctive, "To-morrow, Philip must either sin or not sin": (1) the assertion of Philip's sinning to-morrow involves the denial of his not necessarily sinning; (2) the denial of Philip's sinning to-morrow involves the assertion of his necessarily not sinning.

No logician can admit that this second pair of propositions contain formally the same statements as

the first pair. Nor will the adequacy of the first analysis be questioned by any one acquainted with formal
logic. Therefore the second analysis is incorrect, and
the attempt of Hobbes to draw a proof of necessarianism out of the formal law of excluded middle is a
pronounced failure.

The two members of a disjunctive proposition are
like two balls flung into the air, with a string connec-
ting them. Each ball is fastened, and yet both balls are
loose. Each member of the disjunction is declared necessary, hypothetically upon the denial of the other; yet
neither member is vouched for as being tethered with
an absolute necessity. This must be, if that is not; and
that, if this is not. We do not say: *This must be,* simply:
nor, *That must be,* simply. The disjunctive form is no
evidence for or against the absolute necessity of either
member of the disjunction. Hobbes's argument is perhaps confuted more plainly by this similitude of the
two balls tied together, than by the distinction of *determinate* and *indeterminate,* or even *tityrice* and *tupatulice.*

JOHN LOCKE

JOHN LOCKE

*An Essay concerning Human Understanding
Book II, Chap. XXI. Of Power*

I

"SO far as a man has power to think or not to think, to move or not to move, according to the preference or direction of his own mind, so far is a man free."

It is characteristic of Locke as a writer to refuse to acknowledge difficulties. Where other philosophers check their pace, and tread warily, and whisper in one another's ear that they are drawing nigh to a very grave question, Locke flies forward with a bound, and overpowers the question, and beats it down low, and lays the answer open, as he declares, to any ordinary understanding. This procedure has its advantages. Difficulties in metaphysics, as in government, in trade or in travel, are often creatures of the imagination. The remedy in such cases is to act and cease to imagine. Still there are difficulties, real difficulties, on every line. To ignore them is not to surmount them, but to bequeath them to posterity. When Locke sought to silence the strife about the real essences of substances by proclaiming them unknowable, he left it for Berkeley and Hume in the next generation to ask whether substance had any real essence at all. So the award just pronounced by him on the question of free will is plain and intelligible; but I fear it is also irrelevant and superficial, and quite fails to touch the point at issue. The strife between necessarians and libertarians precisely concerns that preference or direction of his own mind, which Locke assumes. How does the mind prefer thinking of a thing to not thinking of it? How does the mind direct movement rather than rest? Does it prefer or direct in such a way as that it could not possibly prefer or direct otherwise? This is the question to which necessarians answer yes, and libertarians no; and which Locke's definition of freedom touches not at all.

In proof of the insufficiency of the definition, let me show that it applies to cases of the most rigid necessity. A clock is in no sense a free agent. Yet a clock might be called free when it has power to move or not to move, according to the preference and direction of its own workings. It would then be free from all extraneous, all "anti-horological" interference, such as that of a child gluing the fingers to the dial or playing with the weights. Locke, I know, speaks, not of the workings of a machine, but of the direction of a man's own mind; and he refuses, rightly enough, to recognise any liberty away from mind. But is not this the point in dispute, whether our minds are wound up like clocks, to prefer and direct us to certain motions, or whether, they have a command over themselves, placed in themselves alone, which machines have not? If the latter is the true idea of freedom, Locke's definition fails to convey it.

II

"Wherever any performance or forbearance are not equally in a man's power; wherever doing or not doing will not follow equally upon the preference of his mind directing it, there he is not free, though perhaps the action may be voluntary. . . Suppose a man to be carried, whilst fast asleep, into a room, where is a person he longs to see and speak with, and be there locked fast in, beyond his power to get out; he awakes, and is glad to find himself in so desirable company, which he stays willingly in, i.e., prefers his stay to going away. I ask, is not this stay voluntary? I think nobody will doubt it; and yet, being locked fast in, 'tis evident he is not at liberty not to stay; he has not freedom to be gone."

Let me too cite an imaginary instance. Suppose a man's mark to be required to a paper in order to the perpetration of a fraud, and another seizes his hand, and by overpowering constraint traces with it the mark required; and the man whose hand is held, though he cannot help himself, makes the mark with a hearty good will. I ask, is not the man thus constrained a defrauder? I do not mean a defrauder before the law, for the law takes cognisance only of the outward act, which is here evidently constrained, but a defrauder in conscience and before heaven? I think nobody will doubt it; and yet, his hand being held, it is evident that he is not at liberty not to make the mark, he has not freedom to withhold it. How then is his action wrong, if he does it not freely? It is not so much the action as the act that is wrong. The physical action of marking the paper must be performed by him whether he will or no, and none can blame him for that his hand is forced; but the mental act by which he approves of the marking is an approval which he might have withheld, which he freely bestows, and for which God holds him culpable. The man who affixes his mark under such circumstances is at once a voluntary agent, and a free agent, and a guilty agent; voluntary, because he wills what he does; free, because he need not have willed it; and guilty, because he freely wills to do a fraudulent thing.

III

"If this be so, as I imagine it is, I leave it to be considered whether it may not help to put an end to that long agitated, and, I think, unreasonable because unintelligible question, viz., whether man's will be free or no. For if I mistake not, it follows, from what I have said, that the question itself is altogether improper; and it is as insignificant to ask whether man's will be free, as to ask whether his sleep be swift, or his virtue square; liberty being as little applicable to the will as swiftness of motion is to sleep, or squareness to virtue. Every one would laugh at the absurdity of such a question as either of these, because it is obvious that the modifications of motion belong not to sleep, nor the difference of figure to virtue. And when any one well considers it, I think he will plainly perceive that liberty, which is but a power, belongs only to agents and cannot be an attribute or modification of the will, which is also but a power. . . For can it be denied that whatever agent has a power to think on its own actions, and to prefer their doing or omission, either to other, has that faculty called will? Will then is nothing but such a power. Liberty, on the other hand, is the power a man has to do or forbear doing any particular action, according as its doing or forbearance has the actual preference in the mind, which is the same thing as to say, according as he himself wills it."

A rambler in a hilly country will come sometimes upon a sheet of water, sombre, still and solemn, which partly from its own appearance, and partly from the ideas of size impressed by the heights around, he will judge to be very deep. He tries the experiment of going into it, and finds it a shallow with a bottom of black mud. And so the reader of Locke's great work, when he arrives at the striking passage just quoted, a passage that marks an epoch in the free will controversy, is seized with awe, and doubts not, as well from the reputation of the author as from the originality of the statement, that the reasoning which underlies it must be profound indeed. But when the first surprise is over, if he coolly proceeds to reduce the wondrous argumentation into form, another wonder will start up, how the shallow sense therein contained can have passed with so many readers for deep discernment.

Locke's definitions of will and freedom may be given as follows:

Will is power of thinking on one's own actions, and preferring their doing to their omission, or their omission to their doing.

Liberty is power of doing or forbearing to do any action, according as its doing or forbearance has the actual preference in the mind.

Which definitions amount to these:

Will is power of choosing.

Liberty is power of acting according to choice.

From which definitions it follows that this proposition,
The will has freedom (or)
The will is free,
is equipollent with this:

The power of choosing has the power of acting according to choice.

But that proposition is absurd, since one power cannot have another power. Therefore the proposition, "The will is free," is absurd, unintelligible, meaningless and irrelevant, or, as Locke says, insignificant and improper.

This is Locke's line of argument, and no one can deny that the conclusion of it does follow from the premisses, which are definitions. But as one definition is wrong and the others defective, the whole argument must be said decidedly to halt. These are the definitions that I would substitute for them.

Will is power of consciously rejecting evil and choosing good.

Freedom is the not being under constraint to reject any but sheer evil, or choose any but sheer good.

So that the proposition, "The will is free," means:

The power of consciously rejecting evil and choosing good is not under constraint to reject any but sheer evil, or to choose any but sheer good.

There is sense, I contend, in this proposition, whether it be true or not.

Therefore I demand that to the proposition, "The will is free," there be restored that intelligibility, significance and relevance which Locke has unwarrantably denied to it.

Free will is a power, the same power as the will, as

St Thomas shows,* but the liberty or freedom of the
will is not a power but an incident of a power: it is
annexed to the condition under which the power of
rejecting evil and choosing good is exercised; which
condition is this, that sheer good must not be rejected,
nor sheer evil chosen. Sheer good to a person is that
which thoroughly meets the requirements of his nature;
and sheer evil that which meets those requirements in
no way whatever. But the objects with which the human
will is ordinarily conversant are neither sheer good nor
sheer evil: they are good and evil mixed: they partly
satisfy us and partly not. In the not being tied fast to
such objects of choice that liberty consists which is
incident to the faculty or power called the human will.

IV

"We may as properly say that 'tis the singing faculty sings, and the dancing faculty dances, as that
the will chooses, or that the understanding conceives.
. . . I think the question is not proper whether the will
be free, but whether a man be free."

Is not the question, 'whether a man be free to will'?
Instead of debating that, Locke inquires whether a
man be free to do what he wills. For, he asks, how
can we think any one freer than to have the power to
do what he will?

Of course it is the man himself that sings with his
singing faculty, dances with his dancing faculty, chooses
with his will, and conceives with his understanding.
Still we rightly say that the will chooses and the understanding conceives, while we do not say that the

* Sum. Theol. 1, q. lxxxiii, artt. 2 and 4.

6

singing faculty sings, or that the dancing faculty dances. The reason is not far to seek. Will and understanding are faculties, answering to the Aristotelian δύναμις: they are primitive powers. But dancing and singing are not 'faculties,' as Locke is pleased to call them, but habits, the Aristotelian ἕξις: they are acquisitions of skill. Faculty is more intimate to man than habit; and therefore, putting the part for the whole, we take that part for the whole which is more representative of the whole; and speak of the faculty doing what the man does with the faculty.

V

"It passes for a good plea, that a man is not free at all, if he be not as free to will, as he is to act what he wills. Concerning a man's liberty, there is yet raised this farther question, whether a man be free to will; which, I think, is what is meant when it is disputed, whether the will be free. And as to that, I imagine that, willing or volition being an action, and freedom consisting in a power of acting or not acting, a man in respect of willing or the act of volition, when any action in his power is once proposed to his thoughts, as presently to be done, cannot be free. The reason whereof is very manifest: for, it being unavoidable that the action depending on his will should exist or not exist; and its existence or not existence following perfectly the determination and preference of his will; he cannot avoid willing the existence or not existence of that action. It is absolutely necessary that he will the one or the other, i.e., prefer the one to the other; since one of them must necessarily follow, and that which does follow follows by the choice and determination of his mind, that is, by his willing it: for if he did not will it, it would not be. So that, in respect of the act of willing, a man in such a case is not free: liberty consisting in a power to act or not to act, which, in regard of volition, a man upon such a proposal has not. For it is unavoidably necessary to prefer the doing or forbearance of an action in a man's power, which is once so proposed to his thoughts: a man must necessarily will the one or the other of them, upon which preference or volition, the action, or its forbearance, certainly follows, and is truly voluntary; but the act of volition, or preferring one of the two, being that which he cannot avoid, a man in respect of that act of willing is under a necessity, and so cannot be free; unless necessity and freedom can consist together, and a man can be free and bound at once. This then is evident, that in all proposals of present action a man is not at liberty to will or not to will, because he cannot forbear willing: liberty consisting in a power to act or to forbear acting, and in that only."

At last Locke stands at bay before the real question, and dispatches it with a reason which he calls *very manifest*, but which to me appears very obscure, and, on inspection, very inconclusive. I subjoin an analysis, which anyone may compare with the text. Three arguments are given, or rather, three confused statements of one argument: that being Locke's custom when he feels that he has not quite hit the nail on the head, to hammer all about the spot.

First Argument

1. Every action dependent on a man's will must either take place or not take place.

2. Every action dependent on a man's will takes place on condition that he wills it, and does not take place on condition that he does not will it.

3. Therefore the man must will that the action should take place, or will that it should not take place.

Second Argument

1. Every action dependent on a man's will takes place by his willing it: for if he did not will it, it would not be.

2. But he must will one way or the other.

3. Therefore, one way or the other, he wills of necessity.

Third Argument

1. He who cannot forbear willing is not at liberty to will or not to will.

2. Man cannot forbear willing, upon any proposal of present action.

3. Therefore man is not at liberty to will or not to will upon any proposal of present action.

The first remark that I have to make upon these arguments is that they need lengthening out in order to reach the heart of the matter of free will. If they are valid, they prove that, when an action is proposed to us, we must either positively consent or positively refuse to do it: we are not free to abstain alike from consent and refusal. But some, I suppose, contend that this conclusion still leaves us free; since, though we must exert an act of the will, it rests with us, they say, to make that act a consent or a refusal. Though I do not agree with those thinkers, their position, it seems to me, has enough show of reason to render Locke's triumph incomplete until it is rebutted. But I deny that conclusion (that we are not free to abstain alike from consent and refusal), and challenge the arguments alleged on its behalf.

In the first argument the first proposition is true by virtue of what logicians call the law of excluded middle. The first half of the second proposition is true by the wording. The second half of that same proposition is true as it stands: it is true that the condition for an action, dependent on a man's will, not to take place, is that he shall not will it to take place. But it is not true that the condition for the action not to take place is that he shall positively will its not taking place. That is what Locke wishes to be understood in the second half of this seemingly self-evident second proposition. And that is the false conclusion which he gathers, with a *therefore* prefixed, in the third proposition.

Surely, there is a difference between the negative state of not willing and the positive act, *I will not*. There is a difference between not saying yes and saying no. There is a difference between not voting for a measure and voting against it. When an action depends on my willing it, that is, making up my mind that it shall be done, my refraining from having any will, or making up my mind at all upon the matter, is quite enough to bar the action. I need not say, *It shall not be;* it will not be unless I say, *It shall.* Otherwise there would be no such thing in the world as irresolution. A man who did not at once resolve on one course would thereby have resolved on the other. Yet, who has not been ir-

resolute, undecided, unable to make up his mind, a
prey to hesitation and doubt, in many a critical hour of
his life? It may be replied, however, that this state of
doubt consists, not in a withholding of the will, which
Locke argues to be impossible, but in a quick succession of contradictory volitions. Is irresolution a state
of rest or of oscillation? Oscillation it is called by a
common figure of speech. The figure is so far correct,
inasmuch as a person in doubt inclines now to one
alternative and now to another. But does he will now
the one, now the other? I think he does not will in the
full sense of the term. For what is it fully and properly
to will? I conceive the process to be this. A good is
presented to the mind: a complacency is raised thereby: the person adverts to his complacency, and so ac-
quiesces in it. Now, if I am not mistaken, an irresolute person does not ordinarily accomplish a series of
these processes in full. The advantages of one alternative strike him with a liking for it, but, as he looks
inward, he does not approve of that liking; then come
the rival advantages, and affect him in the same way,
without his taking to them either. Thus he advances to
the first stage of volition on this side and on that, but
on neither side does he reach the second stage. I am
not denying that he may reach it and then go back;
but I say, so far as I can read my own consciousness
on the matter,—and each man has no other consciousness to read but his own,—that a man, when he hesi-
tates, does not usually accomplish in succession a number of complete conflicting volitions; he does not usually
make up his mind fully for a thing and then fully against

it; but he does what the word *hesitate* signifies, he *sticks fast* half way in the process of willing; and the thing which depends on his will is not done, simply because he never thoroughly wills it. If this be so, the fact is fatal to Locke's argumentation.

The second argument is a restatement of the first. The first prosposition in it is true; the second is false, and the conclusion does not follow.

In the third argument, again, the first proposition is true, and the second false, and so the conclusion fails.

VI

"To ask whether a man be at liberty to will motion or rest, speaking or silence, which he pleases, is to ask whether a man can will what he wills or be pleased with what he is pleased with, a question which I think needs no answer; and they who can make a question out of it must suppose one will to determine the acts of another, and another to determine that, and so on *in infinitum*."

To suppose a man already to will or to be pleased with a thing, and then ask whether he can will it or be pleased with it, is of course absurd; but to say that no reason can be assigned for a man's freely willing a thing beyond his freely willing it, is, I believe, to speak the truth. Locke thinks that it involves an infinite series of wills. A man wills because he wills to will, and he wills to will because he wills to will to will, and so forth; but this is absurd; therefore, a man has no self-determination. In like manner it might be argued that we have no self-knowledge; because, if we had, we should say, we know that we know, to infinity. Cardinal Newman remarks on this point:

"Of course these reflex acts may be repeated in a series. As I pronounce that 'Great Britain is an island,' and then pronounce 'That "Great Britain is an island" has a claim on my assent,' or is to 'be assented to,' or to be 'accepted as true,' or to be 'believed,' or simply 'is true' (these predicates being equivalent), so I may proceed, 'The proposition "that Great Britain is an island is to be believed," is to be believed,' etc., etc., and so on to *infinitum*. But this would be trifling. The mind is like a double mirror, in which reflections of self within self multiply themselves till they are undistinguishable, and the first reflection contains all the rest."*

When an offer is made to an antiquarian of a trip to Constantinople, and he is delighted with the idea, that delight does not originate there and then with him. It is the result of the words addressed to him working upon his previous dispositions. The only way in which he personally has promoted the delight which he feels is by those his previous acts which have disposed him that way. But during that first instant of surprise and pleasure he is quite passive. And yet the volition to visit the city of Constantine is already drawn up, like a document awaiting his signature; or to use a more appropriate comparison, it lives already within him, and expects his recognition and acknowledgement of it for his own. Suppose that when he looks into himself he approves of

* *Grammar of Assent*, p. 188.

the complacency which he finds there, and fully and freely wills to undertake the journey, I ask what moves him to that free volition? And the answer is twofold, partly regarding the volition and partly the freedom of it. The volition, by which I mean here the original complacency taken in the idea of actually going to Constantinople, is, as I have said, the result of an impression from without encountering certain previous habits of mind in him who receives it. Thus far the motion comes from without, and not from the person's own self. But the freedom of the volition,— that is, the fact of the complacency being persevered in after advertence, when it might have been rejected, that perseverance is of the proper motion of the person and proceeds from him, and from none other besides him. If you raise the question why he perseveres, you are liable to the demand, why should he not? The complacency has possession of his mind, and we know whence it came. To acquiesce in it and consciously to sustain and intensify it, now that it is present, is not to turn the act in a new direction, but to stamp it with a new character, and, as it were, to set the seal of the *ego* upon it. Clearly, therefore, the person can acquiesce in that complacency. It is no less clear that he need not acquiesce therein. For no nature need acquiesce in what does not fully satisfy its needs. But the needs of man's nature rise as high as does his conception of good; and he conceives good far higher than going to Constantinople. That good, therefore, does not necessitate him to acquiesce in the cmoplacency which it excites within him. If he withholds acquiescence, the complacency, being adverted to without being approved, withers away.

Once more I have explained what I believe to be the process of free volition. The account is open to criticism, as all accounts of delicate workings are. But I do not see how the reproach of postulating an infinite series of wills can be fastened upon it by a candid reader.

VII

*"Good and evil, present and absent, 'tis true, work upon the mind; but that which immediately determines the will from time to time to every voluntary action is the uneasiness of desire fixed on some absent good, either negative, as indolency to one in pain; or positive, as enjoyment of pleasure. That it is this uneasiness that determines the will to the successive voluntary actions whereof the greatest part of our lives is made up, and by which we are conducted through different courses to different ends, I shall endeavour to show both from experience and the reason of the the thing. When a man is perfectly content with the state he is in, which is when he is perfectly without any uneasiness, what industry, what action, what will is there left but to continue in it? Of this every man's observation will satisfy him. . . Convince a man never so much that plenty has its advantages over poverty, make him see and own that the handsome conveniences of life are better than nasty penury, yet as long as he is content with the latter and finds no uneasiness in it, he moves not; his will never is determined to any action that shall bring him out of it. Let a man be ever so well persuaded of the advantages of vir-

* In this quotation the several passages stand not exactly in the same order in which Locke presents them.

tue, that it is as necessary to a man who has any great aims in this world, or hopes in the next, as food to life; yet till he hungers and thirsts after righteousness, till he feels an uneasiness in the want of it, his will will not be determined to any action in pursuit of this confessed greater good; but any other uneasiness he feels in himself shall take place and carry his will to other actions. . . If we inquire into the reason of what experience makes so evident in fact, and examine why 'tis uneasiness alone operates on the will and determines it in its choice, we shall find that, we being capable but of one determination of the will to one action at once, the present uneasiness that we are under does naturally determine the will, in order to that happiness which we all aim at in all our actions; forasmuch as whilst we are under any uneasiness we cannot apprehend ourselves happy or in the way to it; pain and uneasiness being by every one concluded and felt to be inconsistent with happiness, spoiling the relish even of those good things which we have, a little pain serving to mar all the pleasure we rejoiced in. And therefore that which of course determines the choice of our wills to the next action will always be the removing of pain, as long as we have any left, as the first and necessary step towards happiness. Another reason why 'tis uneasiness alone determines the will may be this: because that alone is present, and 'tis against the nature of things that what is absent should operate where it is not. It may be said that absent good may by contemplation be brought home to the mind and made present. The idea of it, indeed, may be in the mind, and viewed as present there; but nothing will be in the mind as a present good able to counterbalance the removal of any uneasiness which we are under till it raises our desire, and the uneasiness of that has the prevalency in determining the will. Till then, the idea in the mind of whatever good is only there like other ideas, the object of bare, inactive speculation, but operates not on the will, nor sets us on work. . . For the removal of the pains we feel and are at present pressed with being the getting out of misery, and consequently the first thing to be done in order to happiness; absent good, though thought on, confessed and appearing to be good, not making any part of this unhappiness in its absence, is jostled out to make way for the removal of those uneasinesses we feel, till due and repeated contemplation has brought it nearer to our mind, given some relish of it, and raised in us some desire, which then beginning to make a part of our present uneasiness stands upon fair terms with the rest to be satisfied, and so according to its greatness and pressure comes in its turn to determine the will. . . Were the will determined by the views of good, as it appears in contemplation greater or less to the understanding, which is the state of all absent good, and that which in the received opinion the will is supposed to move to and to be moved by, I do not see how it could ever get loose from the infinite eternal joys of heaven, once proposed and considered as possible. . . This I think anyone may observe in himself and others, that the greater visible good does not always raise men's desires in proportion to the greatness it appears and is acknowledged to have, though every little trouble moves us, and sets us at work to get rid of it. The reason whereof is evident from the nature of our happiness and misery itself. All present pain, whatever it be, makes a part of our present misery; but all absent good does not at any time make a part of our present happiness, nor the absence of it make a part of our misery. If it did, we should be constantly and infinitely miserable, there being infinite degrees of happiness which are not in our possession. All uneasiness, therefore, being removed, a moderate portion of good serves at present to content men, and some few degrees of pleasure in a succession of ordinary enjoyments make up a happiness wherein they can be satisfied. . . . But we being in this world beset with sundry uneasinesses, distracted with different desires, the next inquiry naturally will be, which of them has the precedency in determining the will to the next action. And to that the answer is, that ordinarily which is the most pressing of those that are judged capable of being then removed. For the will, being the power of directing our operative faculties to some action for some end, cannot at any time be moved towards what is judged at that time unattainable. That would be to suppose an intelligent being designedly to act for an end only to lose its labour; for so it is to act for what is judged not attainable, and therefore very great uneasinesses move not the will when they are judged not capable of a cure: they in that case put us not upon endeavours. But these set apart, the most important and urgent uneasiness we at that time feel is that which ordinarily determines the will successively in that train of voluntary actions which make up our lives. The greatest present uneasiness is the spur to action that is constantly felt and for the most part determines the will in its choice of the next action."

Locke says that the will is determined *ordinarily* and *for the most part* by the greatest present uneasiness: he does not say *always*. Indeed in the next section he sets a limitation to the axiom. With that limitation I shall have to deal. My argument here is not directed against the position upon which Locke ultimately retires, but against the bare, unqualified statement that the will is ever and always determined by the greatest present uneasiness.

And first let us take the word *determined* literally, in the full Hobbesian sense of *necessitated*. Man would be a pitiful creature if he were thus the puppet of his discomforts, the sport of the first uneasiness that befell him. From the cradle to the grave he would grovel in unredeemed bondage to his bodily wants. The cravings of appetite are our earliest promptings to action; and throughout life they touch us closest, and affect us most urgently in the way of present uneasiness. What room does such a doctrine leave for any formation of habits of temperance and self-control?

I wonder what was the greatest present uneasiness of the martyr St Lawrence on his gridiron. His liberation rested with himself: it was to be bought with a word. There was the pain of future remorse in the scale against that word of apostasy: there was the pain of actual burning fire making for it. Which was the greater pain? Some may argue from the martyr's choice, that he found the remorse more painful. But it is not a question of the agony of remorse against the agony of burning, but of a prospect of the former agony against an actual endurance of the latter. It is hard to believe that the shadow of threatened remorse distressed the young deacon more than did the reality of present fire. It is a revolting philosophy which pictures a witness of CHRIST unto torments and death, as merely doing after all the pleasantest thing that he could do under the circumstances, seeking his greater ease and comfort in the jaws of the flames, and only not denying his LORD because on the whole it was less painful to confess Him. It is not creditable to natural manliness, let alone to supernatural sanctity, to be driven by the prickings of uneasiness, as it were at the bayonet's point, to deeds of heroism and high renown.

Or, taking the word *determined* in a looser sense, shall we say that the greatest present uneasiness is ever for the time being the strongest *determinant*, or motive, to the will, whether the will consent to it or not? That would be to ignore the well-established Aristotelian distinction between pleasures that presuppose a previous uneasiness, now being allayed, and pleasures that are attractive of themselves, no uneasiness being presupposed. These are Aristotle's words:

They say that pain is a falling below the natural level, and pleasure a filling up to the natural level. But these are bodily incidents. If pleasure is a filling up to the natural level, the subject of pleasure will be that subject in which the filling up takes place, namely, the body. But that conclusion is not acceptable. Pleasure then is not a filling up, but the man feels pleasure when the filling up takes place. This belief seems to have arisen from the consideration of the pleasures and pains connected with nutrition; seeing that when men are in want of food, and have experienced the previous annoyance of hunger and thirst, then they feel pleasure in the making up of the deficiency. But this is not the case in all pleasures. The pleasures of mathematical discovery involve no such previous pain; nor the pleasures of the senses of smell, hearing and sight; nor the pleasures of memory and hope.

It is not to allay any personal discomfort, or mental uneasiness, that the astronomer sweeps the heavens

with his spectroscope and speculates on the composi-
tion of the stars. Or does the poet sing to allay the
turmoil of a frenzied mind? Keble, I know, maintains the
affirmative in his once-celebrated *Prælectiones Academicæ*.
But there is a poetic and artistic pleasure of a softer
and a gentler sort which comes of an activity congenial
in itself, and attractive to the will for its own sake,
apart from any uneasiness which it may allay.

I further observe that the axiom in debate fails to
allow for force of character, apt to withstand immediate solicitation, and for that habit of endurance of
uneasiness which Aristotle calls καρτερία. For this,
however, Locke himself does make due allowance, as
will appear in the next section.

Happiness on earth is rather prospective than present:
it lies in hope and exertion, not in fruition and repose.
To a huntsman in an eager chase, the very toil of
riding is pleasure. The stoppage of his horse would vex
him more than the escape of the fox. All happy men
on earth are huntsmen after something. This continued
chase supposes a spur of uneasiness, unfelt in the heat
of pursuit, but goading the flank of the eager soul the
moment the pursuit is stopped. We may be at our ease,
after a fashion, so long as we are diligent; but like the
swimmer in troubled waters, we are not, cannot in this
world, be at rest. If then we take "uneasiness" to
include not bodily discomfort only, but the uneasiness
of curiosity, of ambition, of zeal, we must allow that
uneasiness sets an edge on all human motive, though
it would not be true to say that all human motive is
made up of uneasiness. The philosophy of uneasiness

is eloquently set forth by St Augustine, in the two following passages, which seem in place here.

Need is the mother of all human actions. Brethren, I have just told you the truth in brief. Run through in mind any action you like: see if aught engenders them but need. Consider even those pre-eminent arts which are rated high, the pleadings of oratory and the aids of medicine,—for such are the professions which excel in this world,—what of them? Take away lawsuits, whom does the advocate assist? Take away diseases and wounds, what does the physician heal? Again, all those actions of ours that are required and performed for our daily sustenance spring out of need. Ploughing, sowing, planting, navigation, what begets all such works but need and want? Take away hunger, thirst and nakedness, and what use are they all? The same even with the works of mercy that are enjoined in the Christian law. For the works which I have hitherto mentioned are morally good indeed, but belong to all men,—I leave out of count the worst sort of works, those detestable works, crimes and enormities, murders, mutilations and adulteries: them I do not reckon amongst human works,—but these lawful works I speak of are born of no other parent than need, the need incident to our fleshly frailty. The like holds true of those works also which I have said are enjoined upon Christians. *Break thy bread to the needy.* To whom breakest thou, where no one hungers? *Gather the needy and harbourless into thy house.* What stranger dost thou entertain, where all dwell in their own country? What litigants dost thou reconcile, where there is everlasting peace? What dead dost thou bury, where there is life eternal? Thou art not there likely to do any of those lawful works that belong to all men. Thou art not likely to do any of the works of mercy: for those *young of the turtle* (Ps. lxxxiii, 3) will then be flown from the nest. To thee I turn, O Prophet. Thou hast already told us what we shall have: *Blessed are they who dwell in thy house.* Tell us now what the blessed shall do, for I see not any needs in that state to impel me to action. Lo, my present speech and discourse is the fruit of need.

7

Shall there be in heaven the like discoursing, to teach the ignorant, forsooth, and to remind the forgetful? Or shall the Gospel be read there in our own country, where the Word of GOD shall be gazed upon in person? Therefore since the Psalmist, desiring and sighing in our name, has told us what we are to have in the country for which he sighs: *Blessed*, he says, *are they who dwell in thy house*, let him tell us what we are to do. *They shall praise thee for ever and ever*. This will be our whole unceasing occupation, alleluia. Let it not seem to you, brethren, that there will be weariness there, because here you cannot endure to be repeating GOD's praises for long; it is need that diverts you from that joy. And considering that a thing is so much the less pleasing for being unseen, if, under the pressure and frailty of our flesh, we praise with such alacrity what we believe, how shall we praise what we shall see! When death shall be swallowed up in victory; when this mortal body shall have put on immortality, and this corruptible body shall have put on incorruption, no one will say, I have been a long time standing; no one will say, I have been a long time fasting, I have been a long time without sleep. For there shall be great stability there; and the very immortality of our body shall then be rapt in the contemplation of GOD. And if now this word which we dispense to you keeps the frailty of our flesh standing so long, what will that joy do for us? How will it change us? For we shall be like Him, since we shall see Him as He is. Being come to be like Him, when shall we fail? where shall we falter? Let us then rest assured, brethren; naught but the praise of GOD and the love of GOD will satisfy us. If you cease from love, you will cease from praise. But if your love shall be unceasing, inasmuch as that beauty without cloy shall be unceasing, have no fear of not being always able to praise Him whom you will always be able to love. Therefore blessed are they who dwell in Thy house; they shall praise Thee for ever and ever.*

So in another place the holy Doctor treats of our present labour and future rest:

* Aug. in Ps. lxxxiii.

Hunger and thirst fight daily: the weariness of the flesh fights against us: the delight of sleep fights: so too does the oppression of it. We wish to watch, and we fall asleep: we wish to fast, and we hunger and thirst: we wish to stand, and we get tired: we try sitting down, and if we sit long, we are at a loss what to do with ourselves. Whatever we provide for our refreshment, there we find a new want. Are you hungry? some one says to you. You answer, Yes, I am. He sets food before you. He sets it there to refresh you: go on with what is set before you. I know you wished to take refreshment: make that your lasting occupation; by doing so, you will find weariness in that which you had provided to refresh you. You are tired with long sitting: you get up and refresh yourself by a walk. Go on with that recreation: you are wearied with long walking and seek again to sit. Find me any way of refreshing yourself that will not exhaust you anew, if you continue in it. What peace, therefore, is that which men have here in face of so many distresses, cravings, wants and wearinesses? That is no true, no perfect peace. What will be perfect peace? This corruptible body must put on incorruption, and this mortal body put on immortality: then the saying shall be fulfilled which is written: Death is swallowed up in victory. Where is, O death, thy victory? Where is, O death, thy struggle? How should there be entire peace where there is still mortality? For of death comes that weariness which we find in all our refreshments. Of death, I say, because we bear a body doomed to die; a body which the Apostle calls dead, even before the separation of the soul: the body indeed, he says, is dead through sin. Go on with much eating: the very act will kill you. Go on with much fasting, and you will die of it. Sit always, refusing to rise, and you will die of that. Walk always, refusing to sit down, you will die of that. Watch always, refusing to sleep, you will die of that. Sleep always, refusing to awake, you will die of that. When, therefore, death shall be swallowed up in victory, these things shall not be, and there shall be peace, entire and everlasting. We shall be in a certain city, brethren. When I speak of it, I am unwilling to end, especially as scandals thicken. Who would not desire that peace whence no friend shall be absent,

whither no enemy intrudes, where there is no tempter, no
mutineer, no divider of the people of GOD, no harasser of the
Church in the service of the Evil One; when the archrebel
himself shall be cast into everlasting fire, and with him, who-
soever sympathises with him, and will not abandon his cause?
There will then, I say, be peace, peace refined and purified,
among the sons of GOD, all loving one another and seeing
themselves full of GOD, when GOD shall be all in all. We shall
have GOD for our common spectacle: we shall have GOD for
our common possession: we shall have God for our common
peace. Whatever it is that He gives us at present, He will be
to us in place of all that He gives: He will be our entire and
perfect peace. This peace He speaks to His people; this peace
the Psalmist wished to hear when he said: *I will hear what
the Lord speaketh in me, for he will speak peace to his people and
upon his saints.**

VIII

"There being in us a great many uneasinesses
always soliciting and ready to determine the will, it is
natural, as I have said, that the greatest and most pressing should determine the will to the next action, and
so it does for the most part, but not always. For the
mind having in most cases, as is evident from experience, a power to suspend the execution and satisfaction of any of its desires, and so all, one after another,
is at liberty to consider the objects of them, examine
them on all sides, and weigh them with others. In this
lies the liberty man has; and from the not using it right,
comes all that variety of mistakes, errors and faults which
we run into in the conduct of our lives and our endeavours after happiness, whilst we precipitate the determination of our wills, and engage too soon before due
examination. To prevent this, we have a power to suspend the prosecution of this or that desire, as every
one daily may experiment in himself. This seems to me

* Aug. in Ps. lxxxiv.

the source of all liberty; in this seems to consist that which is (as I think, improperly) called free will."

The Bodleian Library possesses a copy of Locke's *Essay concerning Humane Understanding*, bearing the date 1690. In the "Epistle to the Reader" the author informs us how he has made various additions to the work as originally published, notably on Book II, chap. xxi, concerning Liberty and the Will. He goes on ingenuously to say: "These are advantages of this edition, which the bookseller hopes will make it sell. . . He [bookseller] has promised to print them by themselves, so that the former edition may not be wholly lost to those who have it, but by the insertion in their proper places of the passages that will be reprinted alone, to that purpose, the former book may be made as little defective as possible." In the Bodleian copy accordingly these additions figure as insertions between the pages. Opposite p. 124 the reader will find the very extract above quoted: it is numbered "§ 47." It is then an afterthought; and, curiously enough, in this afterthought Locke approximates closely to the theory of free will put forward in the present work. Formerly he held that liberty was the power of thinking or not thinking, doing or forbearing, as we wished; now he makes it to be "a power to suspend the prosecution* of this or that desire."

The exercise of this suspensory power is called by Locke 'forbearance'; and he has already told us that "mere forbearances require as much the determination of the will as the contrary actions." To this statement I

* For "prosecution" I should say "ratification."

do not agree altogether. I accept it only with a distinction. Some forbearances require the determination of the
will, others do not. 'Positive' forbearance is a resolution not to do a thing here and now: that resolution is a
determination of the will,—in fact, a volition. But there
are 'negative' forbearances also. A 'negative' forbearance is the very reverse of resolution: it is a state
of irresolution, indecision, hesitation; there is no determination of the will there. Now if Locke would only
recognise these 'negative' forbearances, and admit
that the aptitude of such forbearance is the root of all
human liberty, my contention with him would cease.

I account this passage of Locke highly valuable and
noteworthy. It contains the answer to the inquiry so
often set on foot, whether the will can follow the weaker
motive. It must be remarked that the strength of a
motive is measured in our regard by the direct attention which we pay to it. When one advantage is carefully contemplated, and a greater advantage carelessly
glanced at, that will be in the mind the greater advantage, which is objectively the less. The good that is
considered at any given instant, furnishes the domi-
nant motive for that instant. If any volition be accomplished just then, it cannot but be a volition to follow
that motive and accept that good. But the person may
for the nonce abstain from all volition, unless the good
before him be a perfect good, filling to the brim his
conscious capacity of enjoyment. If the proposed good
comes short of that measure, he may withhold his approval from the complacency which it has caused in
him: he may check his volition midway, simply by not

going on with it. "In this," as Locke appositely observes, "lies the liberty man has; in this seems to consist that which is, as I think," with all deference to so grave an authority, properly "called free will."

When a boat is left high and dry on the beach, if she floats away with any tide, it must be with the tide that is in at the time of her floating. She cannot float away on Monday morning with the tide that went out on Sunday afternoon. It depends on her owners, provided they secure her properly, whether she shall float away with any tide, and if with any, with what tide. Tides are conceivable, which would sweep away any boat left within their reach; but they are of exceptional occurrence. When the tide is in, and the owners do not wish the boat to go out with it, all that they do is not to unmoor her, that is, they do nothing to her. Their liberty as regards the floating of that boat consists in this, that theirs is the decision whether the boat shall or shall not float away with any ordinary tide: if she does float away, they could have hindered her; if she does not, they could have made her. They suspend the floating till whatsoever tide they think good. This is the picture of the case of a person willing. If he exercises any complete volition, in other words, if he consciously approves any complacency, he must approve the particular complacency that is on him at the moment, and not any absent complacency. It rests with him to approve any or none, with advertence; to will, that is, or to abstain from willing. There are good things great enough to fill with rapturous complacency his whole nature, and necessitate his conscious acceptance of them; but such a good thing is *rara avis in terris*. When a person has a complacency, which does not turn it into a full act of the will, all he need do is not to approve of it: he simply lets it go. He may suspend his volition through complacency after complacency, as many as he is not pleased to sanction.

To interfere with this suspension of volition is to interfere with the agent's freedom. When an enthusiast wishes us to say yes or no upon the spot to a proposal of some interest, we are wont to damp his ardour by telling him that we will see. That expression signifies that we will please ourselves, and follow our own determination, more than he is willing to allow us. A thing said or done on the spur of the moment, before we have had time to think, is rather an appendage and sequel to previous volitions than a fresh volition by itself. It is true that indecision cannot last for ever, and when we have hesitated long, the very length of our hesitation precipitates our choice, which is frequently made in a hurry at the end of a tedious weighing of motives. But account must be taken then, not so much of the actual choice, as of the way by which it has been reached, through a continued exercise of liberty. Perhaps King Edward VI consented to Joan Bocher's death in a fit of don't-care weariness of Cranmer's importunity; but how often had the idea of definitively refusing his consent passed before his mind and not been acted upon, or had been acted upon and the act been recalled! His will, though becoming less free as delay became more and more impossible, was free for every instant that his wavering

lasted: the collected freedom of all those instants together gathers round the volition which sent Joan to
the stake.

IX

"Would anyone be a changeling,* because he is
less determined by wise considerations than a wise
man? Is it worth the name of freedom to be at liberty
to play the fool, and draw shame and misery upon a
man's self? If to break loose from the conduct of reason, and to want that restraint of examination and
judgement which keeps us from choosing or doing
the worst, be liberty, true liberty, madmen and fools
are the only freemen: but yet I think nobody would
choose to be mad for the sake of such liberty but he
that is mad already."

It is impossible for man to be so free as not to be
moved by any motives. For man is not complete in
himself; his nature requires things outside of him;
consequently external objects attract his nature and stir
his craving and influence his conduct. The only question is, what motives shall effectually move him. That
depends on himself. He determines which way he
shall go, and he gathers momentum by going, so that
it is not so easy for him to stop when once he is
started. Thus he becomes as we say *addicted*, that is,
bound over, to virtue or to vice, as St Paul tells the
Romans, "Know ye not that to whomsoever ye yield
yourselves servants to obey, his servants ye are whom
ye obey; whether it be of sin unto death, or of obedience unto righteousness? . . . Being made free from
sin, ye were made servants to righteousness. . . When

* An ape.

ye were servants of sin, ye were free in regard to righteousness."* Free will is not given to us to romp and play the fool with, but to choose good, and thereby contract that habit of choosing good which is called virtue. A person who should strive to observe neutrality between virtue and vice, and seek of set purpose to escape entanglement with either in order to preserve his freedom intact, would speedily become the bondslave of vice. For performances always fall short of the ideal standard of good contemplated by the agent. If then the ideal in view be *not too much of goodness*, the result actually achieved is likely to turn out *a deal too much of villainy*. Plato compared the servant of righteousness, the servant of unrighteousness, and the trimmer between the two, to the city of good government, the city of bad government, and the city of no government, respectively. He shows how rapidly the third state passes into the second, from no government to bad government, from anarchy to tyranny. The man of no habits and no character degenerates into a man of bad character and vicious habits. I have no quarrel with Locke here.

X

"Liberty, 'tis plain, consists in a power to do or not to do, to do or forbear doing, as we will. This cannot be denied. But this seeming to comprehend only the actions of a man consecutive to volition, it is further inquired whether he be at liberty to will or no. And to this it has been answered that in most cases a man is not at liberty to forbear the act of volition; he must exert an

* Romans vi, 16, 18, 20.

act of his will, whereby the action proposed is made to exist or not to exist. But yet there is a case wherein a man is at liberty in respect of willing, and that is the choosing of a remote good as an end to be pursued. Here a man may suspend the act of his choice from being determined for or against the thing proposed, till he has examined whether it be really of a nature in itself and consequences to make him happy or no. . . . That which in the train of our voluntary actions determines the will to any change of operation, is some present uneasiness, which is, or at least is always acccompanied with, that of desire. Desire is always moved by evil, to fly it; because a total freedom from pain always makes a necessary part of our happiness. But every good, nay, every greater good, does not constantly move desire, because it may not make, or may not be taken to make, any necessary part of our happiness. For all that we desire is only to be happy. But though this general desire of happiness operates constantly and invariably, yet the satisfaction of any particular desire can be supended from determining the will to any subservient action till we have maturely examined whether the particular apparent good, which we then desire, makes a part of our real happiness, or be consistent or inconsistent with it. The result of our judgement upon that examination is what ultimately determines the man, who could not be free, if his will were determined by anything but his own desire, guided by his own judgement."

These two extracts together form a sort of map of the ground over which Locke has gone and I after him. Let us recapitulate results. Locke's first position was that " he is free who can do what he wills to do." Liberty, taken this way, is one with power. That man is the most free who is the strongest, the ablest, the

best supplied with means for effecting his purpose,
whatever it be. An absolute sovereign, then, a Sesostris
or a Bajazet, would show forth in his person the perfect type of a free man. The plenitude of liberty is the
plenitude of arbitrary power; and Hobbes was right
in his sarcastic observation, that when men cry for
liberty, they want power. I am surprised at a patriarch
of English Liberalism lending any countenance to this
view. What fault had Locke to find with Charles II
and James II, if those aspirants to autocracy were
merely coveting for themselves that which is the birth-
right of every Englishman? Why did Locke place the
German Ocean between him and two such liberty-
loving English monarchs? Was it because they loved
power too well? But if power is freedom, what Liberal
can love it too well? I will desist, however, from this
argumentum ad hominem. I need do no more than remark that power may well be physical freedom, but it
is not that mental and moral autonomy which a psychologist, to say nothing of a statesman, is bound to
study.

Locke's second position was that "the will is determined by the greatest present uneasiness." If that
were true without qualification, there would be no
room for the moral autonomy of free will. Uneasiness
comes upon us from without. It is not ourselves, but
our surroundings, including the accidents of our body
independent of our will, that make us uneasy. Virtue,
or the steady doing of what is right, could never be
secured by these fortuitous promptings of uneasiness.
Happily, most men are virtuous to a greater or less

degree. They could not live within the pale of a civilised community otherwise. Locke recognises this truth; and thereupon endows us with a power to " suspend the satisfaction of any particular desire till we have further considered whether the particular apparent good, which we then desire, makes a part of our real happiness." This third position is a near approximation to what I consider to be the true theory of free will. The one thing that I dislike about it is that Locke takes this suspension to be always itself an act of volition. Were it so, it would be necessary for the philosopher to inquire into the motive of that act of suspension, or the present ' uneasiness ' that determined such act. It would look very much like a resolution taken, a volition achieved, against the greatest present uneasiness. This troublesome inquiry is rendered unnecessary, if we allow that the suspension or adjournment of action need not come of a positive volition to adjourn, but merely out of a negation, the absence of a full self-determination to act. The present ' uneasiness,' as Locke calls it, determines the spontaneous complacency; but that *motus primo primus*, as divines call it, is not an achieved volition; it must be adverted to, and under advertence its drawbacks must appear. Then, without further act, the adverting mind may hesitate to endorse and approve the complacency, and the complacency never becomes a volition till it is approved. To hurry the agent on so fast as to leave no time for advertence or consideration at all, would be to exclude free choice by the exclusion of all choice and full volition. Under the above explanation I agree with Locke that "the man could not be free, if his will were determined by anything else than his own desire, guided by his own judgement."

In conclusion, I observe that it is one thing for an action to be our own by being freely done by us, and another thing for it to be our own by being an action becoming for us to do. An action becoming us may even be somewhat of a necessity on our part. I allude not to the outward constraint of any secular arm, but to the inner efficacy of a virtuous custom. A man who has long studied good and done good, sees evil so clearly to be evil that the horror of evil is the strongest repulsion of his nature. It is not too much to say that he cannot abruptly throw himself into the lap of wickedness. But this inability is not a privation of freedom in any sense in which freedom is valuable. Freedom is naught, except it be riddance of something bad. To be rid of an indifferent thing is no gain: to be rid of a good thing is a loss. *Deliver us from evil* is the prayer which we are taught to offer for freedom.

The evil that haunts the region of the intellect is ignorance, uncertainty and error. A free mind, then, is a mind endowed with a sure knowledge of truth. In one way such a mind is not free: it is restrained from doubt and delusion: it has surrendered to evidence, and evidence holds it captive. In the region of the will dwells the evil of folly. From that the wise man is delivered in so far as he has compassed wisdom. The wiser he grows, the more nearly impossible it becomes for him to do a foolish thing. The one right course to take in every perplexity shines luminously before him. So schooled are his eyes to discern the beauty of that light that he will not, and scarcely can, diverge into the fenny quagmires where the *ignis fatuus* gleams. Is not that a happy impotence, snatching his soul from death and his feet from stumbling? Freedman now of truth and goodness, finds he aught to envy in the licentious rovings of the runaway slave?

It is well, in conclusion, to remark that the blissful dependence of a believer upon truth, and of a just man upon righteousness, is not entered upon without free acts of the will. He alone holds any high practical truth securely who has grasped it resolutely. He alone has any sort of gulf fixed in this world between his will and sin, who in many a circumstance of temptation has had the power to transgress, and has not transgressed, and the power to do evil and has not done it.

DAVID HUME

DAVID HUME

An Inquiry concerning Human Understanding
Section VIII. Of Liberty and Necessity

I

" FROM this circumstance alone that a controversy
has been long kept on foot, and remains still undecided, we may presume that there is some ambiguity in the expression, and that the disputants affix
different ideas to the terms employed in the controversy. . . This has been the case in the long disputed
question concerning liberty and necessity. . . I hope,
therefore, to make it appear that all men have ever
agreed in the doctrine both of necessity and of liberty,
according to any reasonable sense which can be put
on those terms; and that the whole controversy has
turned hitherto upon words."

We hear in this passage the echo of Locke's vehement denunciation of words ill understood, as the
sources whence most disputes in philosophy spring.
But there is yet another fountain-head, whence contention issues in still greater volume. Many differ-
ences amongst philosophers are traceable to words ill
understood, but many more to different aims in life
chosen and pursued. For philosophy is not a bare
speculation; it involves practice. From philosophy are
derived the laws of conduct.

The freedom of the will, if free it be, is a pragmatic
consideration for us all. It is a summons to responsi-

bility, to merit or demerit, to exertion, to fighting, to victory or defeat. It means that we are not embarked as otiose passengers, but we must work our passage through life, and we shall drift to shipwreck if we will not work. Though the LORD is our light and our salvation, we need to follow the light in order to attain salvation. When we have wilfully loved darkness and gone astray, the hope of reaching our destined end dies down in our breasts; we become uneasy and repine at our misconduct, which is exactly the frame of mind wherein a man would gladly hear that there is no free will, and consequently no ground for remorse, no sin. Let the advocates of necessarianism consider what a source of prejudice is here arrayed on their side. Then they will be less hasty in giving judgement that consciousness does not witness to freedom, and that, apart from misunderstandings of language, all mankind are necessarians. *Cui bono fuit?* Whose interest is it to figure as one necessitated in all his actions?

To form a rough guess whether a contradiction between two philosophers is real or verbal, it is well to look whether the two men agree in their practice. If they do, there is reason to hope that their speculations are not really at variance, and that they might be brought to manifest harmony by mutual explanation and definition of terms. But where one disputant takes one line of action, and his opponent acts just the reverse way, there is indication of a conflict of thought, which may be aggravated rather than appeased by a removal of ambiguity of expression.

II

"It seems evident that if all the scenes of nature were continually shifted in such a manner that no two events bore any resemblance to each other, but every object was entirely new, without any similitude to whatever had been seen before, we should never in that case have attained the least idea of necessity, or of a connexion among these objects. We might say, upon such a supposition, that one object or event has followed another; not that one was produced by another. The relation of cause and effect must be utterly unknown to mankind. Inference and reasoning concerning the operations of nature would from that moment be at an end; and the memory and senses remain the only channels by which the knowledge of any real existence could possibly have access to the mind. Our idea therefore of necessity and causation arises entirely from the uniformity observable in the operations of nature, where similar objects are constantly conjoined together, and the mind is determined by custom to infer the one from the appearance of the other. These two circumstances form the whole of that necessity which we ascribe to matter. Beyond the constant conjunction of similar objects, and the consequent inference from one to the other, we have no notion of any necessity or connexion. If it appear, therefore, that all mankind have ever allowed, without any doubt or hesitation, that these two circumstances take place in the voluntary actions of men and in the operations of mind, it must follow that all mankind have ever agreed in the doctrine of necessity, and that they have hitherto disputed merely for not understanding each other."

However irregularly the scenes of nature were shifted, still I think we should not fail to attain some idea of necessity: nay, I am not sure that the idea would not be imprinted upon us even more vividly than it is now. Suppose that, when a man rose in the morning, the floor of his bedroom at first felt like thistles and cut his feet: the moment after it was like smooth glass: then it became a bog, and then a snowfield: suppose that the water with which he tried to wash turned to ink, and then to treacle, and then to oil of vitriol; that the soap burnt his skin and then gilt it; that his stature grew and shrank through all sizes between three feet and thirty; that he took by turns the shape of every animal in the Zoological Gardens; and that changes like these befell him all the days of his life without any regularity of recurrence; still, I am apt to reckon, if he preserved his personal identity, and remained conscious to himself of an enduring self or *ego*, he might attain an idea of necessity, clear and distinct to a degree. For he would live under perpetual constraint. Nature is a stubborn thing for any of us to deal with. Yet we know something of her ways and observances, and can arrange our plans according to them. The man I am supposing would desire and contrive as we do, but, with the protean instruments supplied to his hands, he would be for ever failing of his purpose. Then he would understand what "I cannot" meant. And what else is it to say, "I cannot," but to say, "Necessity is upon me"? "I cannot speak," that is, "I am under a necessity of silence"; "I cannot help it," that is, "I needs must suffer it." We feel the pressure of necessity when we realise the limitation of our being and ability. Now what would a man find himself able to do in a universe where law reigned not? When he hit upon an action that suited his purpose, he would try it again, but the same means might not serve him another time. Then he would desire, and desire in vain: so necessity would make herself felt upon him. Who so necessitous as the impotent?

The state of chaotic irregularity, which we imagined for example's sake, was taken by Plato and his followers to have been the actual state of the universe of matter, before the supreme mind subjected it to law and uniformity. "In those days," says Plato, "nothing had any order except by accident, nor did anything at all deserve to bear any of the names that now are used, such as *fire*, *water*, and the names of the other elements. All this chaos the Artificer first sorted out and made into a cosmos, and then out of it He constituted the present universe."* And again: "God, finding the whole visible universe not at rest, but moving in an unharmonious and disorderly manner, reduced it from disorder to order."† Now the name which the Platonists gave to the primitive principle of capriciousness, irregularity, inconstancy, and variation in nature, was this very name of ἀνάγκη, or necessity. Once more the great founder of the school: "The universe is a compound, the result of a union of necessity and mind... We must distinguish two sorts of causes, the one necessary and the other divine."‡ It is usual to identify freedom with caprice, and necessity with uniformity. But a little consideration will show the reason

* Plato, *Timæus*, 69.   † Id. ib. 30.   ‡ Id. ib. 48, 68.

that there was on Plato's side. It is essential to free will that two men in the same situation should not inevitably make the same choice. Yet if both are equally wise, and both choose for the best, they will in point of fact often choose the same; for frequently there is one best course evident to intelligence. Plato supposed that nature was uniform, in so far as it was swayed by the divine Mind for the best. On the other hand, where there is no mind and no appreciation of goodness, things will fall out blindly, capriciously, irregularly, or, as the Platonist said, by force of necessity, by brute force, the *vis consili expers* of Horace. The Greeks called that "necessity" against which human contrivance was powerless. Now if nature were not anywhere uniform, human contrivance would be powerless everywhere.

We might then have an idea of necessity, even though nature were not uniform. But nature is uniform. Is then Hume right in saying that "our idea of necessity and causation arises entirely from the uniformity observable in the operations of nature"? What is our idea of necessity, according to Hume? He assigns two notes to that idea, "the constant conjunction of similar objects and the consequent inference from one to the other." Uniform conjunction prompting inference makes necessity, says Hume. Happily for mankind, Hume is wrong. Happily for mankind, I say: for were this analysis correct, it would be a bar to all progress in the arts of life, and to all amelioration of man's life on earth consequent upon such progress. Let us consider for example the progress of surgery. Fifty years ago certain injuries were uniformly conjoined with death, and death might be inferred from the receiving of such injuries. If surgeons had been guided by Hume, they would have acquiesced in the necessity of death in such cases; they would have avowed the impossibility of cure, and, says Aristotle, "When the impossible is come upon, men desist."* But enterprising and inventive men took another course. "True," they said, "in the past people always have died of these injuries, but that is no reason why they always should die: what always has been, need not be: past uniformity does not make necessity." They tried new conditions, novel treatment, extra precautions, and patients recovered. The necessary then is not what always has been, but what in the nature of things must be: the two ideas are not the same. Necessity is not constant conjunction, but implication.

For a conjunction that always is, belongs to the actual order of fact; but a conjunction that must be, appertains to the ideal order of possibility. A and B may ever coexist, as the earth and moon coexist, and yet the idea of one does not include the idea of the other: they may be separated in thought, though in fact they will not be separated: their separation is an intelligible hypothesis. On the other hand, were A and B necessarily connected, the having them apart would be a contradiction in terms: A without B would not be A, and B without A would not be B, the one supposing the other. No conceivable arrangement then could separate the two.

* *Eth. Nic.* i.

Such is the necessary connexion between a natural effect and the causes that lead to it. When any material agent acts, the action absolutely must be as it is. Not only does the moon always draw after it the tidal wave, it cannot do otherwise than draw it. For the moon and the earth to be as they are without interference, and yet for there to be no tide, is an hypothesis that cannot be expressed without simultaneous assertion and denial of the nature of the two bodies. As the hypothesis is self-contradictory, so is the thing absolutely impossible. Of course an arrangement might be devised to prevent the tides, but that would not be the present arrangement. GOD Himself, if He wished the tide not to rise, would not leave things exactly as they are, without altering or adding to the forces now in operation. As things stand, supposing no change in their position, and no new force, natural or preternatural, brought to bear, the tide must rise, it cannot but rise, it rises not only invariably and uniformly, but of a necessity.

By 'necessary' therefore I understand that which cannot but be. I proceed to examine whence this notion is derived. It is not gathered from the study of external nature alone, for, as Hume strongly urges, the utmost which that study directly and by itself teaches is that which always is. If all our knowledge was got by looking outside of ourselves, I doubt whether we should have any idea of necessity, or of active causation, or even of being. Hume in this argumentation tacitly assumes that our knowledge is entirely procured by looking outwards. On the unsound support of that assumption the whole weight of his reasoning rests. Let me repeat his words. He says that if nature were not uniform, "inference and reasoning concerning the operations of nature would from that moment be at an end, and the memory and senses remain the only channels by which the knowledge of any real existence could possibly have access to the mind." Whence I gather that under present conditions, where nature is uniform, the only channels by which the knowledge of any real existence can possibly have access to the mind are the senses, the memory, and inferences and reasoning concerning the operations of nature. The senses, I presume, convey to us impressions of what is outside of us, the memory reinstates those impressions, and the reason sorts and arranges them, like with like. Meanwhile, what is become of ourselves? Have we no knowledge of ourselves? or is self-consciousness a sensation,—of what sense? Do we see or hear or taste or smell self, or feel self with the *sensory papillæ* of our fingers, or is the *ego* an organic sensation like a stomach-ache, or a feeling of expanded muscular energy such as a mower feels in cutting a swathe? Or perhaps we remember ourselves. But how can we remember that which we have not first apprehended? And if self is not any operation of nature, and our reasoning is only about operations of nature, I am at a loss to conceive how we can attain to a reasoned knowledge of self. And yet somehow we do know self. We could not make *I* the subject of so many certain asseverations, if *I* were an unknown quantity or a meaningless name. But how the meaning is discovered in Hume's detail of the mental powers does not appear.

Therefore, besides memory and the senses and reasoning about nature, we must mention self-consciousness as another "canal" by which "the knowledge of real existence" has "access to the mind." It is along this canal, if I mistake not, that the idea of necessity travels most of its way. The following are utterances of consciousness: *I am, I do, I can, I cannot, I cannot but*. In all these instances we have self speaking to self on the present state of self. It is not maintained that these truths of consciousness are recognised antecedently to all experience. However it may be with pure spirits, in man certainly the *ego* is not adverted to as a being and a power till after many a feeling has entered in at the gates of the senses. Nor are we aware of what we can do and what we cannot before we have tried. But when we try and the effort is in vain, in that position we are conscious of inability, and we know that there are changes which we cannot bring about. When we cannot bring about a change, we are fain to let things remain as they are. Thus we are conscious of *I cannot but*,—that is, *I must, I am under a necessity*. From *I must* the transition is easy to *you must, he must, it must*. Here is the idea of necessity arrived at by means of consciousness of self, working concomitantly with experience of nature; in other words, by the measurement of self against nature. The uniformity of nature is irrelevant to this process. Were nature a disorderly flux of changes, supposing self to be constant, we should still battle against the external chaos, and still appreciate *I cannot* and *I must*. Of course, if self were fluxional likewise, we should not gather the idea of necessity. But neither should we gather any other idea, for there would be an end of *us*.

We learn to pronounce brute nature necessitated by marking it off from and contrasting it with our own intelligent and free selves.

III

"It is universally acknowledged that there is a great uniformity among the actions of men in all nations and ages, and that human nature remains the same in its principles and operations. . . Nor are the earth, water, and other elements examined by Aristotle and Hippocrates, more like to those which at present lie under our observation, than the men, described by Polybius and Tacitus, are to those who now govern the world. . . We must not, however, expect that this uniformity of human actions should be carried to such a length, as that all men in the same circumstances will always act precisely in the same manner, without making any allowance for the diversity of characters, prejudices and opinions. Such a uniformity in every particular is found in no part of nature. Thus, for instance, in the human body, when the usual symptoms of health or sickness disappoint our expectations; when medicines operate not with their wonted power; when irregular events follow from any particular cause; the philosopher and physician are not surprised at the matter, nor are ever tempted to deny in general the necessity and uniformity of those principles by which the animal economy is conducted. They know that a human body is a mighty complicated machine, that many secret powers lurk in it which are altogether beyond our comprehension, that to us it must often appear very uncertain in its operations, and that, therefore, the irregular events which outwardly discover themselves can be no proof that the laws of nature are not observed with the greatest regularity in its internal operations and government. The philosopher, if he be consistent, must apply the same reasoning to the actions and volitions of intelligent agents."

Hume's argument forms a syllogism to this effect: Necessity is the constant conjunction of similar objects, and the consequent possibility of inference from one to the other: but such a conjunction and potential inference obtains in human volition: necessity, therefore, obtains in human volition. The major premiss of this syllogism I have combated in the previous section. I have now to consider the minor, in proof whereof Hume alleges this fact, that human nature is the same in all ages, a fact not wholly unquestioned by the modern anthropologist. "Ambition, avarice, self-love, vanity, friendship, generosity, public spirit, these passions," says our author, "mixed in various degrees and distributed through society, have been, from the beginning of the world, and still are, the sources of all the actions and enterprises which have ever been observed among mankind." Suppose that this enumeration of human motives is complete, it follows that men have the same sort of inducements to action now as they had three thousand years ago: it does not follow that the same inducement uniformly begets the same action. Plato tells of an Athenian

citizen, who taking a walk along the wall that joined
Athens with the Piræus, came to the place where the
bodies of criminals were exposed to public view after
death. Curiosity impelled him to go and have a look;
and, on the other hand, respect for self and for humanity, that peculiar feeling which the Greeks call αἰδώς,
prompted him to avert his gaze and pass by. At last
he stretched his eyes wide open with his hands, and
rushed to see the sight, saying to his eyes: "There
now, ye wretches, take your fill of the fair spectacle."
An Englishman, placed to-day in the like circumstances, would likewise be attracted by curiosity and
repelled by αἰδώς : his character in all essential points
might resemble that Athenian's. But that he would
act in the same way, and that every one else, similarly
circumstanced and disposed, would do the like, is an
assumption that requires proof, other proof than the
mere showing that they would all have the same inducements for action.

An inducement is a motive upon which a person
may act. If the motive is strong, he probably will act
upon it. If it is overpowering, he must act upon it.
We observe motives of various degrees of strength
influencing men. We can estimate, more or less accurately, the power of a certain motive in a certain mind;
and often we can decrease or diminish it to serve our
purpose. Thus far the actions of our fellow-men are
submitted to our calculation and control. Society could
not go on otherwise. But that this calculation is always
certain, and this control in every respect entire, is a
position that no necessarian has dared to maintain.

Necessarians undertake to show why volitions are not as amenable to our calculation as eclipses, and on the supposition that volitions are in themselves as calculable as eclipses, their explanation is excellent. But since the absolute calculability of volitions is just the point in dispute, their argument falls under that frequently employed form called *petitio principii*, in which the defects of the premisses are made good by begging what should have been proved. From the fact that men are influenced by motives, it follows that human actions can be calculated to a certain extent; and so experience shows that they can. From the libertarian doctrine that men are not necessitated by motives, it follows that human actions cannot be calculated with universal certainty: neither is there any experience of any such certain and universal calculation. It appears that experience so far squares well with libertarian conclusions. No evidence for necessarianism can be got from theorising upon facts which are just as well explained on the hypothesis of free will.

But I am told that the success hitherto attained in calculating human action forms only a fragment of the proof of necessarianism, and cannot fairly be criticised apart from the main argument. That argument runs as follows: Where we have been able to get data and to handle them, our calculations have never failed: we have had experience of this in a sufficient number of instances to warrant an induction, to the effect that all results are calculable, given the data and the calculating power: we find the volitions of men calculable to some extent, which is so far in our favour, and on the strength of the above-mentioned induction we declare that the exceeding multitude and variety of the antecedents to volition alone prevents us from determining accurately in all cases the result which uniformly and necessarily follows. This argument is confirmed by the example of the weather. In the present state of knowledge, the weather is in some ways less predictable than the actions of men: so that when a man is unusually wayward and unreliable we call him a weathercock. A whimsical observer might thence take occasion to assert free wind and free sunshine: and he might show that his theory suited meteorological facts quite as well as did the supposition of an undiscovered uniformity.* Yet even the defenders of free will avow that the assertion of free weather is utterly demolished by the force of the induction already stated. Is not this confession a virtual surrender of the libertarian position? Or take the instance which Hume cites, of a disease which baffles the calculations of the physicians. They do not jump to the conclusion that the patient is afflicted by a free agency. A medical man has had sufficient experience of nature to put faith in the uniformity of her operations, even when it is not apparent to his eyes. Outward irregularity is to him no argument of the absence of inward law, for he knows that "a human body is a mighty complicated machine." Should not the psychologist reason as the physician? Is not the human mind also "a mighty complicated machine"? Why should volition be free

* Room is left for the theory that the weather is subject to occasional angelic interference.

9

any more than the plague of Athens or the earthquake of Lisbon?

In brief, I rejoin that volition is free because it is the act of a mind, and a mind is not a machine. Let us take the induction that is alleged against free will, and try it by the canons of sound inductive proof laid down by Mill. The argument before us is one of the sort which Bacon and Mill call "induction by simple enumeration," where a law is proved by mere accumulation of instances. In that case, it is important that the generalisation should not be extended to regions where the circumstances are unlike those in the midst of which the uniformity has been observed to obtain. Thus from the fact that Roman Catholicism has at no date hitherto been the only religion professed by men, it would be rash to pronounce without further study that Roman Catholicism will not be the only religion on earth ten thousand years hence. We cannot foretell with anything like precision that a child, when he is grown up, will be as we have known him in childhood. The success of a form of government in England is not a sufficient guarantee of its succeeding in Italy. The constitution under which we live and prosper, as our fathers before us, may not suit the temper of our grandchildren. When a certain fact has been noticed over and over again attending another fact, the appearance of one becomes a sign of the other. But if a third fact, momentous and novel, appears upon the scene, the sign may be at fault, and it would be imprudent to rely upon it, till fresh experience has been procured of the altered state of things, or a bringing to bear of previous knowledge has shown that the new circumstance has not affected the character of the sign. To apply this maxim to the case in question. Wherever we have been able to get data, say the necessarians,—or uniformists, if they prefer that name,—wherever we have been able to get data, which have not baffled us by their detail, we have calculated the resultant action unerringly: therefore all actions might be surely deduced from their antecedent causes, supposing a completeness of data and a competent calculating power: therefore, as the movements of a system of weights and pulleys, so might the volitions of man be rigidly calculated from their causes, which are the motives and previous dispositions of the person. But, I rejoin, there is one condition of deep significance attaching to the operations of intelligent mind, and not to the operations of matter. This condition, in the libertarian view, renders the action of intelligence a phenomenon *sui generis*, specifically distinct from the phenomena of mechanics, chemistry, biology, and even of mere sensation and animal impulse. This condition is the foundation of free will. In virtue of the presence of this condition it is maintained that the number of instances which would suffice for an induction in the grosser region of matter is not sufficient in the finer domain of intelligence. The condition in question is reflex consciousness, or the power of adverting to one's own mental states and recognising one's own actions as one's own.

If anyone is still disposed to carry on the induction from matter to mind, let him hear the eloquent

language of Ferrier, speaking of "the great and ano-
malous fact of human consciousness," an anomaly
sufficient to dissipate all surprise at what Bain is
pleased to call the " enormous theoretical difficulty,"
the "metaphysical deadlock," the "puzzle and paradox of the first degree," the " inextricable knot " of
free will.* I must premise that by " consciousness "
Ferrier means not direct but reflex consciousness, or
self-consciousness, or what I have termed " advertence."

"And truly this fact is well worthy of our regard,
and one which will worthily reward our pains. It is a
fact of most surpassing wonder; a fact prolific in sublime results. Standing aloof as much as possible from
our acquired and inveterate habits of thought; divest-
ing ourselves as much as possible of our natural pre-
possessions, and of that familiarity which has blunted
the edge of astonishment, let us consider what we
know to be the fact, namely, that existence, combined
with intelligence [?] and passion in many instances,
but unaccompanied by any other fact, is the general
rule of creation. Knowing this, would it not be but an
easy step for us to conclude that it is also the universal
rule of creation? and would not such a conclusion be
a step naturally taken? Finding this, and nothing
more than this, to be the great fact 'in heaven and
on earth, and in the waters under the earth,' would
it not be rational to conclude that it admitted of no
exception? Such, certainly, would be the natural inference, and in it there would be nothing at all surprising.
But suppose that when it was on the point of being
drawn, there suddenly, and for the first time, started

* *The Emotions and the Will,* p. 493.

up in a single Being a fact at variance with this whole analogy of creation, and contradicting this otherwise universal rule; we ask, Would not this be a fact attractive and wonderful indeed? Would not every attempt to bring this Being under the great general law of the universe be at once, and most properly, abandoned? Would not this new fact be held exclusively worthy of scientific consideration, as the feature which distinguished its possessor with the utmost clearness from all other creatures, and as that which would be sure to lead the observer to a knowledge of the true and essential character of the being manifesting it? Would not, in fine, a world entirely new be here opened up to research? And now, if we would really behold such a fact, we have but to turn to ourselves and ponder over the fact of consciousness; for consciousness is precisely that marvellous, that unexampled fact which we have been here supposing and shadowing forth."*

IV

"And indeed, when we consider how aptly natural and moral evidence link together and form only one chain of argument, we shall make no scruple to allow that they are of the same nature and derived from the same principles. A prisoner, who has neither money nor interest, discovers the impossibility of his escape, as well when he considers the obstinacy of the gaoler, as the walls and bars with which he is surrounded; and, in all attempts for his freedom, chooses rather to work upon the stone and iron of the one than upon the inflexible nature of the other. The same prisoner, when conducted to the scaffold, foresees his death as certainly from the constancy and fidelity of his guards, as from the operation of the axe or wheel.

* Ferrier's *Remains*, vol. II, pp. 87, 88.

His mind runs along a certain train of ideas: the refusal of the soldiers to consent to his escape; the action of the executioner; the separation of the head and body; bleeding, convulsive motions and death. Here is a connected chain of natural causes and voluntary actions; but the mind feels no difference between them in passing from one link to another, nor is less certain of the future event than if it were connected with the objects present to the memory or senses by a train of causes cemented together by what we are pleased to call a physical necessity. . . . A man who at noon leaves his purse full of gold on the pavement at Charing Cross, may as well expect that it will fly away like a feather, as that he will find it untouched an hour after. About one half of human reasonings contain inferences of a similar nature."

Here is further proof of the minor premiss of the syllogism which was put forward in the previous section. I admit, of course, that human behaviour is frequently matter of inference. The admission in no way militates against free will, as may appear by the enunciation of two simple principles, which I call the principle of habitual volition and the principle of averages. A word upon each.

The principle of habitual volition may be stated thus: a person who has his mind already made up to do a thing, need not make it up afresh when the moment for action comes. It is enough that he clings to his habitual purpose; to which, if it is firm, and especially if it has been frequently carried out in deed, he will cling, unless some novel and extraordinary motive arise to deter him. If, therefore, we know that a person has made up his mind, and has no special motive for unmaking it, we may reckon, with more or less probability according to the circumstances of the case, that he will act up to his resolve. This may be most confidently anticipated, when a number of men are publicly pledged to a common course of external behaviour: for there the force of example operates to prevent individual defection.

Thus the gaoler, that Hume speaks of, has determined not to let his prisoners escape. He did that when he first entered into office, and long practice has confirmed him in his determination. It is now a matter of course with him to keep men in prison. He never thinks of doing otherwise, except in extraordinary circumstances. As the prisoner in this case " has neither money nor interest," his circumstances are not extraordinary. The gaoler in guarding him does not form a new act of will: his will is fixed already, and takes effect accordingly, there being nothing to unfix it. When in the beginning he undertook the charge of prisoners, he did specially will to keep them, and that volition was free. His detention of this prisoner, the three-hundredth perhaps that he has lodged, is a sequel to that volition, and may be reckoned surely to follow from such an antecedent in the absence of uncommon motives. The case is the same with the soldiers on guard at the execution. They, too, are acting out a previous resolution, which they have no temption to break. Military discipline largely consists in an acquired readiness to act automatically. But though their performance of military duty in ordinary cases may be presumed from the fact of their being in the army, disciplined to obey, and moving as one man under the binding spell of sympathy and example, yet their being in that state is the result of acts of individual volunteering and free choice, which could not be calculated.

I pass to the enunciation of the second principle, the principle of averages.

When from a knowledge of motives we can form a probable anticipation of the behaviour of every individual out of a large body, we possess a practically certain foreknowledge of the behaviour of the generality, which certitude becomes more indefectible as the body is more numerous.

This is the foundation principle of the sciences of human action. The statesman and the public economist are not concerned to decide what this or that particular man will do; their concern lies with the behaviour of the masses. Of them they can be sure: of the individual they cannot, and care not to be. I bring an example, which I single out because it has been urged as irreconcilable with any theory of free will.*
Suppose the building trade becomes more lucrative than the rest, at once it draws capital from the other trades, until the equilibrium of profits is restored. This occurrence may be looked for as confidently as the motion of water to its level, though the latter is a physical and the former a moral phenomenon. Still no just suspicion is cast on the free will of the capitalist, who

* By Bain, *Emotions and Will*, p. 495, quoting from Samuel Bailey.

rushes into bricks and mortar. The determination to
turn builder is not absolutely calculable in the case
of an individual speculator. But it is calculable for the
generality, on the principle of averages, without prejudice to the freedom of the individual.

When this formidable instance has been met, the
purse at Charing Cross presents little difficulty. I should
be loth to leave any purse of mine in so exposed a
situation, except on the motive which Diogenes had
in throwing his money into the sea, to get rid of it.
The speedy removal of such a purse is certain. The
police have their instructions in such cases; and need,
greed, or curiosity might necessitate some wills. But
the removal might be accounted for without allowing
that any will was necessitated thereto. The first passer-
by, that was not a philosopher, would feel a violent
inclination to take the purse, and probably would take
it. Probability always conquers in the long run; and
here, with the probability so high, there would be no
long run.

V

"It would seem indeed that men begin at the wrong
end of this question concerning liberty and necessity,
when they enter upon it by examining the faculties of
the soul, the influence of the understanding, and the
operations of the will. Let them first discuss a more
simple question, namely, the operations of body and of
brute unintelligent matter."

If man were not a person, he would not be free. By
a person I mean a being who realises in consciousness
that which is expressed in language by the first per.-

sonal pronoun, the English I. That act of consciousness is the fountain-head of liberty. It is wanting in
brute animals, and freedom is not in them. It might
have been also wanting in the paragon of animals.
Without self-consciousness man might not indeed have
formed general concepts, or spoken rational language;
but he could have constructed steam-engines, and laid
down railways, and reared palaces for hotels, and
piloted floating cities through the ocean. He might have
done these things as the bee builds her honeycomb and
the beaver his dam without knowing on what principle
they were done, or reflecting on himself as the doer of
them. Let only instinct of the same kind that guides
the beaver and the bee be given in fuller measure to
man, and the material triumphs of which this age is so
proud might all be achieved, without intelligence or
language, without self-consciousness or free will, by
beings in an everlasting state of infancy, not knowing
the difference between good and evil, between their
right hand and their left. Moreover, a utilitarian kind
of morality might be established among such subli-
mated beavers. When Beaverman A, prompted by glut-
tony, in the course of the uniform sequence of action
upon motive, partook of more meat and drink than
was consistent with the good of united Beaverdom,
the rest of the beaver brotherhood, alike obedient to
their motives, might muzzle their greedy kinsman for
a while, or draw one of his teeth, or otherwise pain him,
so that the recollection of what he had suffered should
counterpoise his appetite in the next temptation. It is
true that actual mankind do the like of this, when

they lock up a drunkard or whip a garrotter. It is true that the bees on Hymettus built in some respects as well as the men on the Acropolis. It is true, but it is not the whole truth. The vice of the phenomenal, uniformist, or positive philosophy lies not so much in what it affirms as in what it denies or overlooks. Thus it lays stress on points of agreement between man and brute, and slurs over what is much more important and valuable, the points of contrast. Abstraction, language, self-consciousness, these facts have slight justice done them by positivist observers. One might think that the school was so named because they posit the facts that suit them, and suppress whatever their philosophy is incompetent to explain. Else they might have considered that, when man is punished, not only is physical pain inflicted, as in the beating of a horse, but also a moral reproach is cast, a stigma and brand of guilt. Also, in comparing the doings of brute animals with the doings of men, they might have contrived to escape a little while from the cloud of anecdote, and examine in the serenity of their own hearts how men act with consciousness of themselves as authors of their action; thence they might have gone back to inquire of the brutes whether they too possessed self-consciousness, and whether there was any grunt of a pig, or bark of a dog, or neigh of a horse, or other cry of any brute animal whatsoever, that could be taken to mean *I know what I am doing*.

The dependence of free will on personality has been often declared. A number of my companions go to a place: I feel ashamed to be left behind: so I am dis-

posed to go too. So far my state of mind involves no
personal or free act. If the willing process in me were
completed there, as it is completed in other gregarious
animals, I could not help going, I must needs go: liberty
to do otherwise would be out of the question. But I
advert to my disposition, and in that advertence of self
to self, in that conscious personal act, my liberty begins.

In the light of this explanation let us view the sug-
gestion of Hume, that men begin at the wrong end of
the question of liberty when they enter upon it by an
examination of the soul, the understanding and the will,
without a previous study of body and brute matter.
I remark that, though Hume speaks of beginning with
matter, his reasoning not only begins with matter but
ends there. He asserts certain facts and lays down certain laws about the operations of brute agents, and thence
proceeds to extend those laws to intelligent agents, as
though there were no new facts in the case. Is intelligence a fact so attenuated and insignificant that no proof
even of its insignificance is required? *Ama valde intel-
lectum*, is St Augustine's advice: the sceptic Hume will
not throw on intelligence even a passing glance, and
that where the inquiry lies concerning the mode of
action of an intelligent being. First appearances condemn such inattention to fact: the subsequent discovery that the fact so neglected is the cardinal point of
the case, excludes the argument from further hearing.
The operations of body and of brute unintelligent
matter may be the right end to begin at in this question of liberty and necessity, but assuredly it is the
wrong end to stop at.

In a good course of education the science of matter is taught before the science of mind. Youths should learn something of geometry, mechanics, astronomy, chemistry and physiology, before advancing to psychology and metaphysics. The very derivation of the name "metaphysics," μετὰ τὰ φυσικά, points to this procedure. The rule is to proceed from the more simple to the more complex. In this order, geometry superadds extension to the number that was treated of in arithmetic: mechanics superadd force upon extension: astronomy contemplates a particular disposition of forces: chemistry superadds upon force that which is known as chemical combination; and physiology upon chemical combination superadds life. And beyond physiology ranks psychology, the object-matter of which is not simply a living organism but a conscious mind. This being the order of precedence in time amongst the sciences, a student would defeat the end for which that order is framed, if his mind refused to take on new facts in his progress from science to science. Suppose in mechanics he would attend to nothing but extension, without regard to force, which of the phenomena of motion could he investigate to any purpose? Could he, on grounds on pure geometry, arbitrate the difference between Newton and Descartes as to the motor power in the heavens? Could he discuss spontaneous generation on mechanical principles? Mechanical, or even chemical, biology is looked upon unfavourably by good judges of science. What, therefore, should be thought of a mechanical, unconscious, impersonal psychology, and physical renderings of moral action ? Such explanations are at best incomplete; and when they profess completeness, they become positively erroneous.

VI

"The necessity of any action, whether of matter or of mind, is not, properly speaking, a quality in the agent, but in any thinking or intelligent being who may consider the action; and it consists chiefly in the determination of his thoughts to infer the existence of that action from some preceding objects; as liberty, when opposed to necessity, is nothing but the want of that determination, and a certain looseness or indifference which we feel in passing or not passing from the idea of one object to that of any succeeding one. Now we may observe that, though, in reflecting on human actions, we seldom feel such a looseness or indifference, but are commonly able to infer them with considerable certainty from their motives, and from the dispositions of the agent; yet it frequently happens that, in performing the actions themselves, we are sensible of something like it: and as all resembling objects are readily taken for each other, this has been employed as a demonstrative and even intuitive proof of human liberty."

With the exception of some volitions of men and angels, all things that happen in nature, all bodily and mental actions of creatures, are necessary actions, actions that cannot but follow upon their antecedents, that is to say, upon the sum of relevant conditions, positive and negative, going before. This attribute of the actions, that they cannot but ensue under the circumstances, is their necessity. Surely it is an attribute of the actions themselves, wholly independent of any

human inference. Whether men infer it or not, the
action ensues and cannot but ensue. The sequence and
its inevitability together make an objective fact. The
necessity, Hume says, is "a quality in any intelligent
being who may consider the action: it consists chiefly
in the determination of his thoughts to infer, etc." No,
it is that which determines his thought to infer, and
that is no quality in him, but in the object which he
is studying. For however much he may determine his
thought to infer the sequence of the action, the action
will not ensue unless there be that in the object which
is of itself adequate to determine a well-informed mind
to infer the sequence. According to Hume, necessity
is confidence in inferring, and liberty is hesitation in
inferring. Then the necessity of the orbit of the moon
lies ("chiefly" at least, for Hume has the caution of
his race) in the confidence with which astronomers
calculate the moon's path in the heavens. Then, if
there were no calculating astronomers, where would
the moon be? To ask such a simple question nowadays is to incur the imputation of "dualism," and to
be taunted with one's ignorance of the great philosopher for whom Hume prepared the way, Kant. To Kant,
of course, necessity is a "form" of the mind. But I
leave Kant alone, and Hume so far as he is Kantian,
as he appears to be in this passage. I may as well avow
that I am a dualist, and hold by "things in themselves."*

There is, however, one case in which the liberty or

* For Necessity as a form of the mind, compare the remarks on
Contingency in my *Of God and His Creatures*, pp. 49, 50, 63, 244,
259. For Potentiality as involving "things in themselves," see ib.
pp. 17, 38, 39.

necessity of an action belongs to the thinking or intelligent being who considers it: I mean when the
action is that being's own. Hume in faltering accents
admits that, though we infer other people's conduct
from their antecedent motives and dispositions, we
are frequently at a loss to infer from those data what
step we ourselves are just about to take. And yet
there, where we are best informed, is just the case
where our prediction should be most confident and
unfaltering. Are we not acquainted with our dispositions by an experience commensurate with our rational lives? How comes it then that we are so much at
fault in the prediction of our own immediately future
behaviour? From this perplexity English philosophers
may extricate themselves by a study of the English
language. Good grammar and sound psychology concur in proclaiming that it is not my business to calculate what I *shall* do, but to decide what I *will* do.
The distinction between *shall* and *will* is overlooked
by Hume, and by necessarians and uniformists generally. No man in adjusting his *will* reasons out his *shall*:
resolution and speculation are two acts incompatible
in the same instant.

VII

"Let any one define a cause, without compre-
hending, as a part of the definition, a necessary connexion with its effect, and let him show, distinctly, the
origin of the idea, expressed by the definition; and I
shall readily give up the whole controversy. . . Had
not objects a regular conjunction with each other, we
should never have entertained any notion of cause
and effect, and this regular conjunction produces that

inference of the understanding, which is the only connexion that we can have any comprehension of. Whoever attempts a definition of cause, exclusive of these
circumstances, will be obliged either to employ unintelligible terms or such as are synonymous to the term
which he endeavours to define. Thus, if a cause be
defined, 'that which produces anything,' it is easy to
observe that 'producing' is synonymous to 'causing.'
In like manner, if a cause be defined 'that by which
anything exists,' this is liable to the same objection.
Had it been said that a cause is 'that after which anything exists,' we should have understood the terms.
For this is, indeed, all that we know of the matter.
And this constancy forms the essence of necessity, nor
have we any other idea of it."

Another quotation, this time from Plato:

"'And don't tell me,' he said, 'that justice is duty,
or advantage, or profit, or gain, or interest, for that
sort of watery stuff won't do for me; I must, and will,
have a precise answer.' . . 'You are a philosopher,
Thrasymachus,' I replied, 'and well know that if you
ask what numbers make up twelve, taking care to prohibit the person whom you ask from answering twice
six, or three times four, or six times two, or four
times three, for this sort of nonsense won't do for me;
then, obviously, if that is your way of putting the
question to him, neither he nor anyone can answer.
And suppose he were to say, "Thrasymachus, what do
you mean? And if the true answer to the question is
one of these numbers which you interdict, am I to say
some other number, which is not the right one,—is
that your meaning?" how would you answer him?'
'Yes,' said he, 'but how remarkably parallel the two
cases are!' 'Very likely they are,' I replied; 'but even

if they are not, and only appear to be parallel to the person who is asked, can he to whom the question is put avoid saying what he thinks, even though you and I join in forbidding him?' 'Well, then, I suppose you are going to make one of the interdicted answers?' 'I dare say that I may, notwithstanding the danger, if, upon reflection, I approve any of them.'"*

I fear I am making one of the answers which Hume interdicts when I define a cause as "that by which aught is made or done." He will observe that "making" or "doing" is the same as "causing." I admit it: it is on that very point that I lay stress. Elementary notions, like "cause," "being," "right," cannot be defined without a certain tautology. But it is better to be tautological than falsely philosophical. Better is a familiar definition than one which surprises and deludes. "That after which anything constantly exists" is certainly no synonym of "cause." It means a great deal less than cause, and applies to a great many things that are not causes: it cannot stand as a definition. It leaves out that notion of "making," or "doing," or "producing," which, on Hume's own avowal, is one with the notion of causing. And it takes in what no reasonable man would venture to call a cause. There is a rainbow at two o'clock, and at six o'clock there is an accident to an excursion train. Did the rainbow cause the accident? No, I say, for it did not make or produce it. "No," Hume cries, "for an accident does not always follow after a rainbow." His definition excludes that case. But it does not exclude the case of

* Plato, *Republic*, Book 1, Jowett's Translation.

night following day, nor of the ebb of the tide following the flow, nor of weakness following strength. Yet
how insufficient an explanation it would be to say that
the sun set because it rose; that the tide went out because it came in, or that a man was weak in old age
because in youth he was strong!

I would draw a distinction between a "cause" and
and an "explanation." By "cause" I understand, as I
have already defined, "that by which aught is made
or done." By "explanation" I understand "that after
which an event always follows and always would follow
under any conceivable hypothesis." I call "explanation" what John Stuart Mill, in his *Logic*, calls "cause,"
and defines to be "that after which a phenomenon
follows invariably and unconditionally," in which definition the adverb *invariably* signifies that the phenomenon always follows; and, *unconditionally*, that it
always would follow. *Unconditionally* is well rendered
by the French *quand même*. This is an explanation in
the sense in which a grammatical construction is said
to be "explained" by quoting a rule of grammar. It
is an alleging of the indefectible law of which the case
in point forms an instance. Thus the phenomenon of
sunset is explicable by a recitation of the facts of the
existence, opaqueness and rotation of the earth, and
of the existence and luminous nature of the sun.
These positive conditions, along with the negative
condition of the absence of arrangements to the contrary,—such as would be a provision for reflecting the
sun's rays round the earth,—are the explanation of
sunset. Suppose all this, and you may suppose what

else you like: the sun surely will set. The negative condition bargains, amongst other things, for the absence of miraculous interposition. If GOD, at the prayer of another Joshua, willed the sun not to set as it usually does, He would make some unusual arrangement against its setting. His would be no barren velleity, leaving the antecedents just as they were, without addition. That would be to will and will not, which is not the way of a wise being. For we must remember that the uniformity of nature, whereby certain consequents are annexed to certain antecedents is GOD's express will and ordinance. "He hath 'stablished it for ever, for ever and aye; he hath given command, and it shall not pass away."

No 'explanation' in the technical sense just defined can be given of the volitions of free agents as such. Of a free act you cannot predicate that it always follows and always would follow any given previous state of things; you cannot particularise the antecedent or set of antecedents upon which such an act ensues invariably and unconditionally. The reason of this anomaly is manifest: it is the addition of personality, of self-consciousness. Here there are not simply facts following facts: there is, to boot, an *ego* reviewing the sequence.

But though, strictly speaking, no 'explanation' is assignable for a free volition, yet every volition has a cause; for every volition is an act, and every act has its doer. The doer of an act of will is the person willing. He it is by whom the act is done; he then is the cause of the volition. The definition of 'cause' here

involved does not comprehend any necessary connexion with the effect. Though it appear a paradox, it
is the truth in regard to volition, that the effect is necessarily connected with the cause, but not the cause
with the effect. If the volition has taken place, the
agent must have willed it; but the agent may be in the
conjuncture proper for willing, and yet no volition
ensue.*

The origin of the idea expressed by the definition,
' A cause is that by which aught is made or done,' is
not far to seek; we find it in our consciousness of ourselves. We recognise ourselves as the principle of our
acts, the source from whence they proceed. We learn
to say, ' I made so and so,' ' I did so and so,' ' Such
and such a work is mine.' But we cannot say this of
everything. We are surrounded with what we have not
made, we are the victims of much that we have not
done. Thereby we are taught to detach the idea of
' maker ' or ' doer ' from the idea of self, and form the
general concept of ' cause.'

To cause is to act, to work, to energise: it is not
simply to go before, as one phenomenon before another. If nothing is real but phenomena, then to be
sure causation does dwindle down to mere sequence
without action. But how absurd the concept of pure
unsubstantial phenomena, manifestations which reveal
no enduring thing to any abiding person, manifestations of nothing to nobody! How shall we account for

* Compare the teaching of the old theologians that the world is
really related to God, but God is not really related to the world;
which means that the world implies God, but God does not imply
the world.—See *Of God and His Creatures*, pp. 82, 83.

that self of ours, which remembers the past, is conscious of the present, and argues the future, being at once historian, witness and prophet? Sure I am that I am no vanishing phenomenon, no fluxional state of consciousness, but a person who leads a continuous life, identically the same person from age to age. And from my own permanence I argue permanence around me, both of persons and things. I am the subject of changes, which modify but do not subvert my being. When I observe changes of which I am not the subject, I find a subject for them in some permanent being outside myself. I cannot believe that the whole of nature, beyond the bounds of myself, consists of pure changes, floating loose and unattached to any lasting underlying things. But if there exist things that last, or noumena, then appearances that pass, or phenomena, are the actions of those lasting things; in other words, noumenal things are the causes of phenomenal changes.

VIII

" Liberty, when opposed to necessity, not to constraint, is the same thing with chance; which is universally allowed to have no existence."

Chance may be defined 'an unforeseen coincidence in some sphere of human enterprise.' We do not call the arrangement of the heavens a chance: that is because we find the host of heaven drawn out antecedently to any undertaking of ours. We call no arrangement a chance arrangement, which we recognise as the usual thing in nature, or see to have been designed by man. But when, looking for one thing, we find another, we call that a chance. Many discoveries in science and art have been made by chance. Excavating for drainage purposes, we ' chance upon ' some prehistoric remains. But coming upon a mound which we select as likely to contain such remains, we do not call it 'chance,' if excavation proves our conjecture to have been correct. To the omniscient Mind there is no 'chance.' 'Chance' is a relative term. Absolutely, or objectively, chance has no existence.

An act of free will may be considered, antecedently to its performance, in the reckoning of some interested looker-on. Either that looker-on has endeavoured to influence the choice of the agent, or he has not. Either again he is acquainted with the agent's character and motives, or he is unacquainted with them. If the observer is quite a stranger to the agent and to the circumstances of his action, what the agent will do is to him ' mere chance.' If he knows the man and his motives, he predicts his action with high probability, subject however, in some cases, to an ' element of chance,' which is traceable partly to the observer's ignorance, but partly also to the agent's free will. If the observer has endeavoured to influence the choice, and the agent chooses accordingly, the exerciser of such influence will not ascribe the action to chance, for this reason that he himself has intended it and laboured to bring it about. If, on the other hand, the agent resists the solicitation, the person so thwarted puts the refusal down to obstinacy or ' cussedness,' terms which point to free will: he never ascribes it to chance.

But an act of free will may be otherwise considered,

not in the reckoning of a bystander, but in the mind and will of the agent himself. So considered the act is as far removed from chance as the poles of the heavens stand asunder. The act is "adverted to," it is "meant," it is "known," "willed," "chosen"; all which expressions denote the very reverse of "fortuitous." Not by chance was it that "the well-beloved Brutus stabbed."

Altogether this attempt to tie up free will with chance, and merge them both in non-existence, appears singularly infelicitous. From one point of view chance is not non-existent, while from another point of view free will is not chance.

IX

"There is no method of reasoning more common, and yet none more blameable, than, in philosophical disputes, to endeavour the refutation of any hypothesis by a pretence of its dangerous consequences to religion and morality. When any opinion leads to absurdities, it is certainly false; but it is not certain that an opinion is false because it is of dangerous consequence. Such topics, therefore, ought entirely to be forborne, as serving nothing to the discovery of truth, but only to make the person of an antagonist odious."

This passage has gathered interest during the century and more which has elapsed since it was written. The first issue which it raises is this: how far have we certainty of faith and religion? If there are certainties of faith and religion, any hypothesis in plain diametrical contradiction with such certainties must, on Hume's own confession, be an opinion that "leads to absurdities" and is "certainly false." That there are certainties in faith and religion is the first and prime point of Catholic belief. But how many people who have not the blessing of Catholic faith hold now to such certainties? I am far from replying, None: I do not know how many, but the number of such persons is rapidly diminishing in intellectual circles.

But an opinion may be not contradictory of faith and religion, but merely "dangerous," as threatening contradiction to come. What such an opinion contradicts is not the religious truth itself, exactly as that stands in its certainty, but some sort of explanation which theologians have given of such truth, some shape into which their private hands have moulded it, some protecting envelope in which they have ensheathed it. Here Hume's saying is true: "It is not certain that an opinion is false because it is of dangerous consequence." One is reminded of the notices to cyclists that now diversify our country roads: *Danger, ride cautiously*. The rider is not bidden to stop and go no further, but to go slow, as it were feeling his way. If he persists in riding at a breakneck pace, he may merit the attention of the police. And a Catholic philosopher or theologian, who pushes "dangerous" opinions recklessly, may be censured by some Roman Congregation, not as a heretic, not necessarily as a teacher of false doctrine, but as a "temerarious" person.

A central certain truth of faith and religion is the doctrine of Providence, that GOD has care of the world. In the Middle Ages this came to be curiously bound up with Ptolemaic astronomy. The heavenly spheres, it was supposed, presided, although not absolutely, over terrestrial events; the *primum mobile* conducted the motions of the heavenly spheres; and an angel by divine command guided and impelled the *primum mobile.** When Copernicanism came to be advocated, and the *primum mobile* denied, the new theory seemed "dangerous" to the doctrine of Providence. There was need to proceed with some caution. The divine government of the world had to be otherwise explained. The readjustment was made, the danger disappeared, the heliocentric astronomy was admitted, and certainty of divine faith in Providence still remained. Not every new opinion that has seemed "dangerous" to faith, has turned out so safe and true as Copernicanism.

But necessarianism, or "determinism" as it is now called, is not merely "dangerous": it is in diametric contradiction with the certainties of Catholic faith, at least when it goes the length of affirming that free will is not merely "highly mysterious," "inexplicable," "hitherto unexplained," but that nothing that can be truly called free will has any place in any spiritual nature whatsoever. The ruin of Catholic devotion is the ruin of Catholic faith. But a thing fundamental in Catholic devotion is sorrow and contrition for sin. "Contrition" is "heart-bruising." It is the heart of a penitent broken with sorrow and self-reproach before a GOD whom too late it has come to know, too late it has come to love; too late as regards the commission of sin, although not too late for forgiveness. Its cry is *mea culpa, mea maxima culpa.* Determinism would change all that. Instead of "my fault," all that it

* St Thomas, *Contra Gentiles*, III, chapp. 77-87: *Of God and His Creatures*, pp. 201, 249.

owns to is "my very great misfortune." "My conduct," it says, "has been bad, harmful, disorderly, vicious, ugly and shameful: but with my inherited proclivities, with my environment, my bodily constitution, my temptations, it was the only conduct of which I was capable: anyone else in my exact position would have done just the same: unhappy man that I am, but who can blame me? My conduct indeed has been condemnable, but who can condemn *me*"? Thus self-reproach is exchanged for self-commiseration. The evil-doer is ashamed of his evil doing, but only as a poor man may be ashamed of wearing poor clothes where he has no others to put on. I need not say that such lamentation over self is not contrition. I need not say that such predetermined swerving from the path of righteousness is not sin.*

The denial of free will has merited the explicit condemnation of the Catholic Church, e.g., in the Council of Trent, sess. 6, can. 5. The denial may proceed on theological grounds, as though the fall of Adam had deprived man of free choice in all alternatives of right and wrong, and made sin a necessity to him; or as though the victorious grace of CHRIST, in some few favoured persons, overbore free will, and necessarily produced works meritorious of heaven. Or the denial may proceed on grounds of mere philosophy, as in Hobbes's and Hume's case, which seems to have been the case also of sundry medieval doctors, notably Wyclif. Wyclif was expressly censured in the Council of Constance for declaring *omnia de necessitate eveniunt.*

* See my *Political and Moral Essays*, pp. 259, 260.

The theological denial of free will makes an essential part of the often condemned heresies of Calvinist and Jansenist. I have no intention of discussing the mind of St Augustine. The mind of that profound thinker, and in controversy somewhat impetuous disputant, is a vast region to explore. I content myself with the remark that no necessarian could have shed the tears of contrition which bedew the pages of St Augustine's *Confessions*.

X

"The only proper object of hatred or vengeance is a person, or creature endowed with thought and consciousness; and when any criminal or injurious actions excite that passion, it is only by their relation to the person or connexion with him. Actions are, by their very nature, temporary and perishing; and where they proceed not from some cause in the character or disposition of the person who performed them, they can neither redound to his honour if good, nor infamy if evil. The actions themselves may be blameable; they may be contrary to all the rules of morality and religion; but the person is not answerable for them; and as they proceeded from nothing in him that is durable and constant, and leave nothing of that nature behind them, it is impossible he can upon their account become the object of punishment or vengeance. According to the principle, therefore, which denies necessity, and consequently causes, a man is as pure and untainted after having committed the most horrid crime, as at the first moment of his birth, nor is his character anywise concerned in his actions, since they are not derived from it, and the wickedness of the one can never be used as a proof of the depravity of the other."

To begin with an *argumentum ad hominem*. Hume here repudiates that philosophy which reduces "being," οὐσία, to "becoming," γένεσις; that philosophy which owns no other reality than states of mind, or "actions temporary and perishing"; that philosophy which discovers in man "nothing that is durable and constant," nothing, therefore, that can be called "the person." But such is the very phenomenalist, or positivist, philosophy, which Hume's sceptical attacks on cognition went so far to introduce. Hume professes a horror of "the principle which denies necessity, and consequently causes," the very things which he himself denies, bringing down necessity to fact, and causes to invariable antecedents. And if upon definite antecedents one definite human act invariably (and therefore, in Hume's explanation, necessarily) follows, the facts of character being reckoned among the antecedents, many of us will not hesitate to declare that "a man is as pure and untainted after having committed the most horrid crime as at the first moment of his birth," at least he is no more guilty than the wolf which worries a six-months-old child: what else could the creature rationally be expected to do? In this incautious writing Hume seems to have exposed the flank of his whole philosophy. The present argument, however, deserves treatment on its own merits. The argument is still current: I have myself heard it on the lips of an eminent lecturer in the University of Oxford. Where it is contended that murder, for instance, is a free act, Hume takes that assertion to imply that there was nothing in the character or disposition of the agent inclining him to shed blood, and that, when the deed is done, there ensues in him no inclination to do the like again, but the act stands isolated and all alone, after the manner of the moment out of time, τὸ ἐξαίφνης, which Plato supposes to be the instant of transition from rest to motion, or from motion to rest.* Hume may open all his batteries upon this position without touching one single defender of free will. We all allow that character has a vast influence on conduct: we only deny that it has an absolutely determining influence upon every single point of premeditated action. Likewise we allow that acts form habits; and character is a sum total of acquired habits and congenital proclivities. Character is more or less permanent; but there is something still more permanent than character: that is the " person, or creature endowed with thought and consciousness," a definition which I thankfully take from Hume. Free will in act is eminently a personal act: it is the rational creature's outpouring of its own vitality; and where the act is evil and vitality is poured out with will and deliberation upon an undue object, the person thereby becomes a more or less wicked person, and so remains until the act is revoked.

A wicked character is a mark of wicked deeds: it is produced by them and reproduces them in turn. The deeds by which such a character is produced are freely done. The deeds which it produces are free less and less as they are multiplied, and as the evil character of the doer is more and more confirmed. A wicked character then is a sure mark of wicked deeds having

* Plato, *Parmenides*, 156d.

gone before, and a probable mark of more to follow. Wicked deeds are a sure mark of a wicked character being at least in course of formation, but not necessarily already formed, a fact which founds the Aristotelian distinction between ἀκρατής and ἀκόλαστος.* Volition, like muscular and nervous energy, with which in man it is essentially connected, tends to run in grooves according as it is exercised. There is nothing incompatible with free will there. Free will is limited, like everything else in man.

XI

"If voluntary actions be subjected to the same laws of necessity with the operations of matter, there is a continued chain of necessary causes preordained and predetermined, reaching from the original cause of all to every single volition of every human creature; no contingency anywhere in the universe; no indifference, no liberty. While we act, we are at the same time acted upon. The ultimate Author of all our volitions is the Creator of the world, who first bestowed motion on this immense machine and placed all beings in that particular position whence every subsequent event by an inevitable necessity must result. Human actions, therefore, either can have no moral turpitude at all, as proceeding from so good a cause; or if they have any turpitude, they must involve our Creator in the same guilt, while He is acknowledged to be their ultimate cause and author. For as a man who fired a mine is answerable for all the consequences whether the train he employed be long or short, so wherever a continued chain of necessary causes is fixed, that Being,

---

* See *Nicomachean Ethics*, vii, 9, or *Aquinas Ethicus*, vol. 1, pp. 170, 171.

either finite or infinite, who produces the first is like-wise the author of all the rest, and must both bear the blame and acquire the praise which belongs to them. Our clear and unalterable ideas of morality establish this rule upon unquestionable reasons when we exa-mine the consequences of any human action, and these reasons must still have greater force when applied to the volitions and intentions of a Being infinitely wise and powerful. Ignorance or impotence may be pleaded for so limited a creature as man; but those imperfec-tions have no place in our Creator. He foresaw, He ordained, He intended all those actions of men which we so rashly pronounce criminal. And we must there-fore conclude either that they are not criminal or that the Deity, not man, is accountable for them. But as either of these positions is absurd and impious, it follows that the doctrine from which they are deduced cannot possibly be true."

This is an objection which Hume urges against himself with a vivacity and force that deserve the best thanks of his opponents. In answer he avows that the difficulty is not to be got over by accepting the first alternative, the position that no human actions are criminal. He finds it as impossible to deny wickedness as to deny pain and ugliness in this world of woe. He says: "Why should not the acknowledgement of a real distinction between vice and virtue be reconcilable to all speculative systems of philosophy as well as that of a real distinction between personal beauty and de-formity? Both these distinctions are founded in the natural sentiments of the human mind, and these sentiments are not to be controlled or altered by any philosophical theory or speculation whatsoever."

As Hume does not deny the criminality of certain human actions while he affirms the necessity of them, one is curious to see by what shift he escapes the second horn of his own dilemma. How ever does he avoid the "absurd and impious position," for so he calls it, of charging the Judge of all the earth with all the wrong done there? He makes his escape in the following characteristic manner:

"The second objection admits not of so easy and satisfactory an answer; nor is it possible to explain distinctly how the Deity can be the mediate cause of all the actions of men, without being the author of sin and moral turpitude. These are mysteries, which mere natural and unassisted reason is very unfit to handle; and whatever system she embraces, she must find herself involved in inexplicable difficulties, and even contradictions, at every step which she takes with regard to such subjects. To reconcile the indifference and contingency of human actions with prescience; or to defend absolute decrees, and yet free the Deity from being the author of sin, has been found hitherto to exceed all the power of philosophy. Happy, if she be thence sensible of her temerity, when she pries into these sublime mysteries; and leaving a scene so full of obscurities and perplexities, return with suitable modesty to her true and proper province, the examination of common life; where she will find difficulties enow to employ her inquiries, without launching into so boundless an ocean of doubt, uncertainty and contradiction!"

There is a certain vulpine humility in all this. But it had been more honest either to admit the objection

as valid and unanswerable, an admission tantamount to
a denial of God,—for a bad god is no god at all; or
else to repudiate that Humian doctrine from which
the whole objection proceeds, that "voluntary actions
be subjected to the same laws of necessity with the
operations of matter."

JOHN STUART MILL

JOHN STUART MILL

Logic, Book VI, Chap. II. Of Liberty and Necessity. Examination of Sir William Hamilton's Philosophy, Chap. XXVI. On the Freedom of the Will

I

"CORRECTLY conceived, the doctrine called Philosophical Necessity is simply this: that, given the motives which are present to an individual's mind, and given, likewise, the character and disposition of the individual, the manner in which he will act may be unerringly inferred; that if we knew the person thoroughly, and knew all the inducements which are acting upon him, we could foretell his conduct with as much certainty as we can predict any physical event. This proposition I take to be a mere interpretation of universal experience, a statement in words of what every one is internally convinced of. No one who believed that he knew thoroughly the circumstances of any case, and the characters of the different persons concerned, would hesitate to foretell how all of them would act. Whatever degree of doubt he may in fact feel arises from the uncertainty whether he really knows the circumstances, or the character of some one or other of the persons, with the degree of accuracy required; but by no means from thinking that if he did know these things, there could be any uncertainty what the conduct will be."

Mill strives to rest his doctrine, which is one with that of Hume, upon experience. But I observe that the experience which he invokes is not any knowledge of fact, but a belief about an unobserved contingency: it is not an experience of what is, but an expectation of what would be in a certain issue which never occurs. No one ever does know any person thoroughly, nor the relative values of all the motives affecting any person's conduct out upon a new field of choice where he has never been tried before, where he cannot proceed by force of habit, where he will have to make up his mind afresh,—the very situation in which, if anywhere, free will must come into play. Even a successful prediction in such a case would prove nothing. The success might be due, three-quarters to shrewdness and the remaining quarter to luck, as when one has backed the winner of the Derby. "Three-quarters to shrewdness," I say, for I admit that a free volition may be predicted with probability. I deny only that it can be predicted with certainty even under the fullest knowledge of antecedent conditions of choice. Not with certainty, because the volition is not essentially contained in those conditions. Against this position Mill alleges "a mere interpretation of universal experience,"—his *interpretation*, to wit, but certainly not his *experience*. As I have shown against Hume, the libertarian interpretation, properly guarded and explained, suits all experienced facts of prediction as well as "the doctrine called Philosophical Necessity." Nothing, then, is thereby proved on either side.

II

"The religious metaphysicians who have asserted the freedom of the will have always maintained it to be consistent with divine foreknowledge of our actions; and if with divine, then with any other foreknowledge."

As religious metaphysicians we speak of "the GOD of the Theist and of the Christian; a GOD who is numerically One, who is Personal; the Author, Sustainer and Finisher of all things, the Life of Law and Order, the Moral Governor; One who is Supreme and Sole; like Himself, unlike all things besides Himself, which are but His creatures; distinct from, independent of them all; One who is self-existing, absolutely infinite, who has ever been and ever will be, to whom nothing is past or future; who is all perfection, and the fullness and archetype of every possible excellence, the Truth Itself, Wisdom, Love, Justice, Holiness; One who is All-powerful, All-knowing, Omnipresent, Incomprehensible."* I am not concerned with the correctness of this representation: my sole purpose is to show that they who believe it to be correct are not committed to the inference that if the freedom of the will is consistent with the divine foreknowledge of our actions, it must be consistent likewise with any other foreknowledge. The foreknowledge ascribed to "the GOD of the Theist and of the Christian" not standing on a level with any other foreknowledge, Mill's argument *a pari* becomes inadmissible.

God is "One, who is self-existing, absolutely infinite, who has ever been and ever will be, to whom nothing is

Grammar of Assent, p. 98.

past or future." He is the perfect realisation of all that can be, filling all bounds of being, filling all space and time, yesterday and to-day and for ever the same, stationary in the plentitude of being. Like His being, His knowledge is measured by eternity; it all exists together, it embraces all time. Whatever things come to be in time, are to God eternally present. His vision ranges from eternity over all things as they are under His unvarying all-pervading gaze.

To us the past and the future, when we know them, are present in their images or in their signs.* But to God they are present in themselves, for they are in Him as in their first principle. We are placed at the

* " If the future and the past are, I would know where they are. And if I cannot yet compass that, still I know that, wherever they are, they are not there future or past but present. For if there also they are future, they are not yet there; if there they are past, they are no longer there. Wherever, therefore, they are, and whatever they are, they are not save in the present. When the past is related truly, it is not the past things themselves that are produced from memory, but words formed from the images of them, like footprints which in passing by they have impressed on the mind through the senses. My boyhood for instance, which is no more, is in the time past, which is no more; but when I con over and tell my impression of it, I am looking at an object in the present time, because the impression is still in my memory. . . When the future is said to be seen, it is not the things themselves which as yet are not, or which are future,—it is their causes or signs perchance, that are seen, which signs already are. . . It is now plain and clear that neither the future nor the past is. Nor is it properly said, There are three tenses, the present, the past, and the future; but perhaps it might properly be said: There are three tenses, the present of things past, the present of things present, and the present of things future. For these are three certain realities in the mind, and elsewhere I see them not; the present of things past, which is memory; the present of things present, which is intuition; and the present of things future, which is expectation."—St Augustine's *Confessions*, xi, 18, 20.

circumference of the circle of which He is the centre.
The instant in which we are is one *now* out of many:
from the divine *now* all *nows* radiate, and it is equivalent to them all. Thus to God there is no foreknowledge or afterknowledge, but simply knowledge of the
present. This knowledge, as applied to actual creation,
receives in theology the name of the "science of vision."
By it God sees,—He sees in the act itself, He does not
calculate from antecedents,—all that He Himself is
freely about to do, or rather is doing, in the way of
creating, working miracles and the like, as also all the
effects that will proceed from natural causes, whether
from the necessary determination of their natures, or
through the use made of them by free agents. God,
looking at a creature, sees its history all at once before
Him, albeit that, to the creature, the facts are evolved
successively. The generation that shall be alive thirty-
five years hence will behold what the ruler of France
at that time does.* They will not calculate his actions
from the motives, they will watch them being done.
Thirty-five years hence is present in the *now* of God.
He is a spectator of what is to go on then.

This is marvellous doctrine. If it were not marvellous, it would hardly be likely to be true of Him whose
name is called Wonderful. But it is not on the mar-
vellousness, nor even on the truth of the doctrine that
I here wish to insist, but on the bare fact that this
is the doctrine of those "religious metaphysicians"
who assert the freedom of the will and maintain it to
be consistent with the divine foreknowledge of our con-

* Written about the year 1872.

duct. Such eternal foreknowledge is a thing without parallel in the human mind. It gives, therefore, no ground for the inference set up by Mill.

III

" It is not the doctrine that our volitions and actions are invariable consequents of our antecedent states of mind, that is either contradicted by our consciousness or felt to be degrading. But the doctrine of causation, when considered as obtaining between our volitions and their antecedents, is almost universally conceived as involving more than this. Many do not believe, and very few practically feel, that there is nothing in causation but invariable, certain and unconditional sequence. There are few to whom mere constancy of succession appears a sufficiently stringent bond of union for so peculiar relation as that of cause and effect. Even if the reason repudiates, the imagination retains the feeling of some more intimate connexion, of some peculiar tie or mysterious constraint exercised by the antecedent over the consequent. Now this it is which, considered as applying to the human will, conflicts with our consciousness and revolts our feelings. We are certain that, in the case of our volitions, there is not this mysterious constraint. We know that we are not compelled, as by a magical spell, to obey any particular motive. We feel that if we wish to prove that we have the power of resisting the motive, we could do so (that wish being, it needs scarcely be observed, a new antecedent); and it would be humiliating to our pride and paralysing to our desire of excellence if we thought otherwise. But neither is any such mysterious compulsion now supposed, by the best philosophical authorities, to be exercised by any cause over its effect. Those who think that causes draw their effects after them by a mystical tie, are right in believing that the relation between volitions and their antecedents is of another nature. But they should go further and admit that this is also true of all other effects and of their antecedents. If such a tie is considered to be involved in the word necessity, the doctrine is not true of human actions; but neither is it then true of inanimate objects. It would be more correct to say that matter is not bound by necessity than that mind is so."

This language is, of course, no more than an echo of Hume (nn. 6, 7). But because it is striking and clear, and is caught up with approval by men of our time, and even by boys, it had better be listened to attentively and judged for what it is worth. Mill teaches that volition does not differ from mechanical action, so far as the invariable and unconditional sequence of consequents upon antecedents is concerned. Let the simultaneous facts, A, B, C, D, and others, be followed by the fact Z. Then, says Mill, whatever be the character of the facts, whether mental or physical, it is certain that wherever A, B, C and the rest go before, without addition or diminution, there Z will come after. Experience may show that Z occurs whether A precedes or not. Therefore A may be left out of the account, as likewise may other antecedents, as B, C, D, for the same reason. But it will be found that some antecedents, such as F and G, cannot be omitted without the result Z failing to appear. These antecedents must be retained. Again, the insertion of some new antecedents, as P, Q, R, may be found to prevent the appearance of Z, even though F and G, and all others whose presence is indispensable, are duly there. The omission of these obstructive antecedents must be bargained for. Let the indispensable antecedents, F, G, etc., be summed under the general expression E, and the impeding antecedents, P, Q, R, etc., under the general expression É. Then the expression E – É will stand for what Mill calls the cause of Z, Z being any fact either of mind or of matter.

Let us take an illustration from each department. And first of matter. A smith takes a piece of iron, heats it red-hot in the forge, and beats it flat on the anvil. The iron becoming flat is a fact or phenomenon of matter. The antecedents to it are the smith's having got up that morning, having had his breakfast, having work to do, having put the iron in the fire, having hammered it,—there are these and other antecedents too numerous to mention. The result is that the iron gets flattened out. Any similar iron would get flattened out in similar circumstances. Even a variation of circumstances, up to a certain point, is compatible with the attainment of the result. That smith, we will suppose, said his morning prayers. But iron will yield to beating, whether the hands that strike it have been previously clasped in prayer or not. GOD rains upon the just and the unjust. On the other hand, if the smith is stricken blind, his blow is likely to fail, and the metal will go unflattened. Thus some conditions are requisite to the effect, and some are superfluous. Further, there are conditions of which the absence is positively required. The hot bar must not be cooled in water, else the beating will make no impression. When all the indispensable conditions are there, and the preventive conditions are all absent, the result, the flattening of the iron, will be brought to pass, —*infallibly*, Mill would say: I should add, *and necessarily*.

Let us pass to a phenomenon of will. A man has gained an important success, something that he imagines will fix his name in history: he has vindicated his country's honour in the field, or amended her constitution at home, or he has come forward in the ranks of her poets, her artists or her men of science: and as he thinks of his achievement, his heart is lifted up within him, as was the heart of Lucifer of old, taking the glory to himself away from GOD. If the person deliberately consents to this movement of vainglory, he commits a sin: so all moralists who recognise the rights of the Creator agree in teaching. If we are to believe Mill, the guilty consent there follows upon the temptation with a sequence as indefectible as the flattening of a hot iron consequent upon percussion. When a smith hammers a bar that has been properly heated, and when there is no interference, natural or supernatural, with the operation, it is incredible to Mill, as it is to every reasonable man, that the shape of the bar should remain unchanged. Suppose now two persons are placed together in the situation of trial which I have described. Their antecedent dispositions, their present motives, arising as well from nature as from grace, are essentially alike in number and in kind. In that case it is simply incredible to Mill that one man should sin and the other remain innocent. Crimes, he thinks, are ruled by the same laws as landslips. One cliff will not stand in the exact situation in which a similar cliff has fallen: neither will Abel ever do right, if placed, with Cain's character, in an occasion similar to that in which Cain has done wrong.

Our author indeed says: "We know that we are not compelled, as by a magical spell, to obey any particular motive. We feel that if we wished to prove that we have the power of resisting the motive we could do so." That wish, he adds with emphasis, would be "a new antecedent." Just as well may it be said that a cliff is not compelled, by any magical spell or natural necessity, to give way under any particular mining operation. If, as you cut away the rock, you judiciously replace it with iron pillars, they will bear up the superincumbent mass as it stood before. Those pillars are new antecedents. Without them, or some support like them, the rock, being undermined, surely will fall. With them, if they are sufficient, it as surely will stand. So, on Mill's showing, a man in temptation surely will sin, unless it occurs to him that it would be a fine thing to show his power of resistance. Without that, or some deterring thought of that sort, his offence is calculable, with mathematical precision, from the occasion given him. But supply him with motive sufficient,—or if you like to speak theologically, with grace sufficient,—to keep him out of sin, and there is no more danger of his yielding to temptation than there is of his sinking through a stone pavement.

We have here a system of necessarianism, rigid as that of any Calvinist divine. The recognition of anything that possibly might be other than what actually is cannot stand with the doctrine of philosophical necessity, taught nowadays by "the best philosophical authorities," as Mill complacently styles himself and friends. The sequence of antecedent and consequent in this system is so close, so invariable, so uniform, as to leave no room anywhere for edging in a *might be*. A bridge has given way with a train upon it. It might not be that the train should not fall into the river. It might not be that the bridge, constructed as it was, should not give way under that pressure. It might not be that the railway officials, with their individual characters and incentives to action, should have had the forethought and energy to prevent the train from going upon the bridge. It might not be that the engineer of the bridge should have constructed it in any other way. It might not be that anything which has happened should have happened otherwise. Everywhere, event follows event with rigid calculable precision, till we come to the primeval arrangement, the original collocation of materials in the universe. That, one is tempted to say, might have been arranged quite differently. But here those self-styled "best philosophical authorities" declare human knowledge to stop short. Nothing, they tell us, can be known as to how the first position of things came about. Then it cannot be known that things might have been arranged in the beginning in any other fashion than as they actually were arranged. Consequently, so far as we know, all that happens is inevitable; what happens not, is impossible; and nothing might have been, or might be, except what has been, is, or shall be. This is what the doctrine of philosophical necessity comes to,—Hobbism, pure and simple.

A "mystical tie," indeed, would that relation be, of which there were no terms! The doctrine that "there is nothing in causation but invariable, certain and unconditional sequence," abolishes the terms of the relation of cause and effect, and cuts the relation afloat to go by itself; this event before, and that event after, no permanent being anywhere. If there is nothing of permanent being in ourselves, and nothing permanent in nature, on what ground do we assert the permanence of any law of nature? Why must the future resemble the past, if nothing of the past stands over into the future? No wonder if "many men do not believe, and very few practically feel," that there is nothing in the universe but a ghostly procession of phantoms going before and phantoms coming behind. No wonder if many men persist in looking for substantial realities, and for ties, "mystical" or otherwise, so long as they are real, that is to say, "real relations" between cause and effect. We divide these substantial realities into *persons* and *things*,—*persons* habitually conscious of self, *things* totally unconscious: dumb animals, who need not here be considered, come in between. A *thing* essentially acts upon whatever comes within the range of its action, as the earth on the moon, the sun on the planets, every particle of matter upon every other particle to which its power extends. The effect of such action is some determination to motion. This action of things is called *transient*, because the term of action lies without the agent. Therefore are things called *inert*, because they do not act within or upon themselves, as it were setting themselves in motion. A *person*, on the other hand,—the only *person* I here speak of is thinking man, as such,—is impressed and acted upon by objects without entering into his ken, and to this impression there is a responsive action from within. This action is *immanent*, for it remains within the agent. This is the act of perceiving and liking, or disliking, and in its first stage this action is necessary, being determined, as determinists truly say, by environment and character. It is only in a further stage, when the *ego* consciously awakes to judge of this spontaneous and necessary like or dislike, that the exercise of free will begins.

Libertarians have this abiding dissatisfaction with Hume and Mill and the modern determinist school, that, as men blinded by physics to everything above the physical and material order, they ignore a vital difference between beings *conscious of the ego* and beings totally *unconscious*, between *persons* in fact and *things*. Still, dissatisfied as we are, we are not surprised: we remember that we are dealing with men who have shut out from their philosophical purview all such concepts as that of substantial, permanent Being and Personality (οὐσία, ὑπόστασις), yea even of Body and Soul, and exercise their speculation solely upon transient states of consciousness (γένεσις, αἴσθησις, πάντα ῥεῖ). Such exclusiveness leaves no place for free will, nor for much else that is valuable in human nature: nay, ' nature ' itself loses all persistency and is carried away in the stream of the definitely and determinately 'be-

12

coming.' On all which ' dissolving views ' see Plato, *Theætetus* 179e–183b.

IV

" I am inclined to think that . . . error . . . would be prevented by forbearing to employ, for the expression of the simple fact of causation, so extremely inappropriate a term as necessity. That word, in its other acceptations, involves much more than mere uniformity of sequence; it implies irresistibleness. Applied to the will, it only means that the given cause will be followed by the effect, subject to all possibilities of counteraction by other causes; but in common use it stands for the operation of those causes exclusively, which are supposed too powerful to be counteracted at all. When we say that all human actions take place of necessity, we only mean that they will certainly happen if nothing prevents: when we say that dying of want, to those who cannot get food, is a necessity, we mean that it will certainly happen whatever may be done to prevent it. The application of the same term to the agencies on which human actions depend, as is used to express those agencies of nature which are really uncontrollable, cannot fail, when habitual, to create a feeling of uncontrollableness in the former also. This, however, is a mere illusion. There are physical sequences which we call necessary, as death for want of food or air; there are others which are not said to be necessary, as death from poison, which an antidote, or the use of the stomach-pump, will sometimes avert. It is apt to be forgotten by people's feelings, even if remembered by their understandings, that human actions are in this last predicament; they are never (except in some cases of mania) ruled by any one motive with such absolute sway that there is no room for the influence of any other. The causes, therefore, on which action depends are never uncontrollable; and any given effect is only necessary, provided that the causes tending to produce it are not controlled. That whatever happens, could not have happened otherwise unless something had taken place which was capable of preventing it, no one surely needs hesitate to admit."

This is a distinct advance upon Hume, who thought (n. 7) that necessity added nothing to mere uniformity of sequence. Mill recognises that it adds an element of what we may call *uncounteractableness*. No doubt Mill is right. Only Mill's position is none the better for this correction of his predecessor; for in Mill's philosophy, as in Hume's, whatever is *actually uncounteracted* is practically and in the concrete *uncounteractable;* and therefore *to happen* and *to happen of necessity* are one.

At Minster Lovel on the Windrush, some fifteen miles west of Oxford, may be seen what remains of the house of Sir William Lovel, the trusted minister of Richard III. In the next reign Sir William took part in a rising against Henry VII, was defeated near Stoke, and never heard of again. Some said that he was drowned in the Trent, but others that he found his way back to his Oxfordshire home, and ensconced himself in one of those hiding-places which in those tumultuous days were an indispensable adjunct to every great mansion. One old housekeeper knew his secret, and she suddenly died. A skeleton, supposed to be Sir William's, was found in the hiding-hole in 1708. We may imagine the unhappy plight of the refugee lord and master of that house. He hears the village clock striking his usual dinner-hour: it does not call him to eat. Twenty-four hours pass away to the solitary prisoner, and forty-eight, and—how many more? Men keep aloof from him, and he cannot go to them: nor do the angels come and minister to him. Nothing is left for the man in that situation but death: inevitably, irresistibly, necessarily, he must die. He may weep or sing, sit or stand or lie down, but he must die. The sun may shine or the rain fall, there may be feasting or mourning in the house, his acquaintance may love him or love him not: happen what will, if he remain in that situation, he must die. And so he did die, and there was no help for him.

Sir William died necessarily, as the case stood. We can readily conceive how it might have stood otherwise, how he might have been discovered in time and had food brought him by some faithful domestic. Let us pass to a case of volition, and clothe the volition in those circumstances which best make for freedom, if volition ever is free. I speak of what I know and where I have experience, in contradiction to blind prejudice and lack of experience, when I say that the most perfectly free volition possible is the choice of a state of life, made according to St Ignatius's "method of election" in the *Spiritual Exercises*. But the particular instance chosen matters not. If any one will not take mine, let him pick another for himself, let us say Wellington's resolution to give battle to Marmont at Salamanca. I follow up the instance which I have taken. It is all-important that the "exercitant's" election be his own. The director of the exercises is warned on

no account to express a preference: nay, so far as may
be, he is not to feel a preference of one state over another for the exercitant's choice; he is not to advise
this choice or that, much less to dictate. He is to allow
the Creator to work alone upon the soul that He has
created. Days of careful thought are bestowed on the
choice. Mere emotion is discounted; prayerful reasoning must decide. The decision is made, and in this case
we will suppose it to be, not to become a priest or
religious, but to go into the army. Wrong or right, it
is a thoroughly free election, the exercitant's own
choice. Now I say, considered in the concrete and
under the circumstances in which it is actually made,
that choice is every whit as uncounteractable, in Mill's
philosophy, and quite as necessary, as the refugee's
death in his hiding-hole. Only by violating your hypothesis, and bringing in discovery where discovery was
none, can you save Sir William's life. Only by altering
the exercitant's character, making him antecedently
more of a churchman by disposition than he actually
was, or by striking him with an alarm that in fact he
felt not, or kindling in him an enthusiasm that in his
breast did not burn, could you, on Mill's showing,
bring that 'exercitant' to choose to be a priest. As
things stood, Mill would say, any choice of the
priesthood in him was quite out of the question and
impossible. Nay, taking a wider view of both positions,
we must avow that it was not in the nature of things,
as they lay from the beginning, for Sir William to be
discovered and saved; nor was it part of the existent
order of nature (and there can be only one order of

nature) for that exercitant to have approached his election in other dispositions or under any other play of motive. Mill would have allowed, I think, the necessity of Sir William's death. Most men would allow it, I should allow it myself. No one who holds by Mill can draw any distinction subtle and potent enough to disallow the similar necessity of that exercitant's choice.

There is a children's story of a certain Dutch ship, which encountered a great storm at sea, whereupon the sailors chose one of their number to tie all the rest fast to the mast and spars. And so that one did. Then he fastened himself up, in such a way that, when the storm was over, he might loose first himself and then his comrades. But the ship happening to give a great lurch, he was turned head over heels, and hung unable to release himself. Thus the whole crew were put to drift at the mercy of the weather. Mill depicts mankind in the plight of these unfortunate Dutchmen. Any man might act otherwise than he does, if he could get fresh motives, which would be forthcoming if anyone else could give them; but every man is tied up in invariable and unconditional sequences like his fellowman: thus the world drifts under the breath of necessity.

This sad consequence results from a too unqualified admission of the principle that "whatever happens, could not have happened otherwise unless something had taken place which was capable of preventing it." Man, in certain cases, could have elicited the mere inward, deliberate act of his will otherwise than as he actually has elicited it, and that apart from anything else taking place, other than what has actually taken

place, antecedently to his willing. Man is the one un-
bound sailor in the ship of the physical universe.

V

"Though the doctrine of necessity, as stated by
most who hold it, is very remote from fatalism, it is
probable that most necessarians are fatalists, more or
less, in their feelings. A fatalist believes, or half believes,—for nobody is a consistent fatalist,—not only
that whatever is about to happen will be the infallible
result of the causes which produce it,—which is the
true necessarian doctrine,—but, moreover, that there is
no use in struggling against it; that it will happen however we may strive to prevent it. Now, a necessarian,
believing that our actions follow from our characters,
and that our characters follow from our organization,
our education and our circumstances, is apt to be, with
more or less of consciousness on his part, a fatalist as
to his own actions, and to believe that his nature is
such, or that his education and circumstances have so
moulded his character, that nothing can now prevent
him from feeling and acting in a particular way, or at
least that no effort of his own can hinder it. In the
words of the sect which in our own day has most per-
severingly inculcated and most perversely misunder-
stood this great doctrine, his character is formed *for*
him, and not *by* him; therefore his wishing that it had
been formed differently is of no use; he has no power
to alter it. But this is a grand error. He has, to a certain extent, a power to alter his own character. Its being,
in the ultimate resort, formed *for* him, is not inconsistent with its being in part formed *by* him as one of
the intermediate agents... We are exactly as capable of
making our own character, *if we will*, as others are
of making it for us. Yes, answers the Owenite, but

these words, "if we will," surrender the whole point, since the will to alter own character is given us, not by any efforts of ours, but by circumstances which we cannot help; it comes to us either from external causes, or not at all. Most true: if the Owenite stops here, he is in a position from which nothing can expel him. Our character is formed by us as well as for us; but the wish which induces us to attempt to form it is formed for us, and how? Not, in general, by our organization, nor wholly by our education, but by our experience; experience of the painful consequences of the character we previously had, or by some strong feeling of admiration or aspiration, accidentally aroused."

The Owenite whom Mill combats is his own veritable shadow; or Mill is the shadow of the Owenite. The attitudes of the two precisely correspond. The Owenite alleges that man's character is formed for him and not by him. Mill answers that we are capable of making our own characters, if we will. The Owenite contends that this "if we will" surrenders the whole point, and Mill ingenuously replies, "Most true." The Owenite lays it down that man has no power to alter his character by his wishing. Mill thinks that he has, to some extent. The Owenite points out that the will to alter our character is given us, not by any efforts of ours, but by circumstances which we cannot help; and Mill hastens to assure him that so long as he stops there he is in a position from which nothing can expel him. Is there any difference between the disputants? Whatever there is comes only to this, that the one would have our characters to be formed for us and not by us; the other both for us and by us. But this difference disappears upon the explanation which Mill affords, that our characters are formed for us "in the ultimate resort," but by us "as intermediate agents." Bearing in mind what Mill adds, that this intermediate agency of ours is determined by "external causes," this explanation is everything that the Owenite could desire. Man starts with an organisation which is none of his contriving: he receives an education, that is, a supply of motives from without, tending to direct him in a certain way: he gets experience of painful consequences which he did not mean to encounter: he also has strong feelings, accidentally aroused. These and the like adventitious determinants are the making of the man's character. Character determined from without, and motive coming in from without, rule the man's every choice jointly. It must be so in the absence of free will.

VI

"To think that we have no power of altering our character, and to think that we shall not use our power unless we desire to use it, are very different things and have a very different effect on the mind. A person who does not wish to alter his character cannot be the person who is supposed to feel discouraged or paralysed by thinking himself unable to do it. The depressing effect of the fatalist doctrine can only be felt where there *is* a wish to do what that doctrine represents as impossible. It is of no consequence what we think forms our character, when we have no desire of our own to form it; but it is of great consequence that we should not be prevented from forming such a desire by thinking the attainment impracticable, and that if we have the desire, we should know that the work is not so irrevocably done as to be incapable of being altered."

To think that we shall not use our power to alter our character unless we desire it, and further that we shall not desire it except in accordance with some invariable sequence analogous to the sequence of a feeling of heat from hot weather, seems to be the very same thing and to have the very same effect upon the mind as thinking that we have no power of altering our character. We shall alter it, perhaps, when the desire of amendment supervenes: well, we will await the desire, and when it comes, float out upon it to repentance and amendment.

It is of consequence what we think forms our character, even when we have no present desire of a reformation. For it is important, as Mill well says, "that we should not be prevented from forming such a desire." But we should be prevented, if we thought that the desire, when it came, would take hold of our minds, as the tide of a log lying upon the beach, without our seconding it, and without our being on the alert to transmute by our conscious sanction the spontaneous craving, the velleity for better things, into a solid and effective purpose of amendment.

VII

"And indeed, if we examine closely, we shall find that this feeling of our being able to modify our own character if we wish, is itself the feeling of moral freedom which we are conscious of. A person feels morally free who feels that his habits or his temptations are not his masters, but he theirs: who even in yielding to them knows that he could resist; that were he desirous of altogether throwing them off, there would not be required for the purpose a stronger desire than he knows himself to be capable of feeling. . . The free will doctrine, by keeping in view precisely that portion of the truth which the word Necessity puts out of sight, namely, the power of the mind to co-operate in the formation of its own character, has given to its adherents a practical feeling much nearer to the truth than has generally, I believe, existed in the minds of necessarians. The latter may have had a stronger sense of the importance of what human beings can do to shape the characters of one another; but the free will doctrine has, I believe, fostered in its supporters a much stronger spirit of self-culture."

Here Mill has imitated the tactics of his admired master, Locke. I have remarked how Locke (n.9) shifts his ground, and without express adherence to free will nearly becomes a libertarian. And it has been observed of Mill, by one of the ablest of his opponents,* that he answers objections by yielding to them, and yet will not resign the pretensions of his school. The present passage, if it means anything, means a withdrawal of the application of the doctrine of invariable and unconditional sequence to the operations of the will. But Mill has not written a book of Retractations.

Let us "examine closely," as he suggests, and according to his description, "the feeling of moral freedom which we are conscious of." When we feel morally

* John Grote, in his *Examination of the Utilitarian Philosophy*. It is an Oxford saying: "The best things in Mill are his admissions."

free, we are conscious, according to Mill, of three facts:
(1) that we are able to modify our own character, if we
wish: (2) that we are masters of our habits and temptations, not they of us: (3) that we could resist habit
or temptation even when we yield to it. The first of
these facts has already been discussed. The wishing, on
which our ability to shape our character is conditioned,
must rest consciously with us: else how can we be conscious of possessing that ability? As for the second fact,
our conscious mastery over our habits and temptations,
the said " habits " and " temptations " are the same as
the "dispositions" and "motives" respectively, which
Mill formerly declared to be the causes whence our
actions flow in uniform sequence. But if the sequence
is uniform, we are not masters of our actions, and therefore not of our habits and temptations: they rule us,
not we them. Indeed this *we* is a new term, not introduced before. Before there were antecedent circumstances followed by consequent acts; now there comes
on the scene a person, a conscious agent, who claims
the acts for his own and disputes the mastery of them
with the circumstances. A transition appears to have
been made from physics to psychology. The third fact
which Mill learns from consciousness is that we can resist
temptation even when we yield to it. The very thing
that libertarians say, and the one thing that they care
to keep to! The great champion of the uniformity of
nature acknowledges free will, he avows that he is conscious of it. Let all that is here written against him be
cast into the fire, and let his literary executors cancel
his chapter on Liberty and Necessity, all except the

present passage; and the little world that reads our books will be delighted with the unusual spectacle of a philosopher come to terms with his adversary. For if in yielding to a temptation we know that we can resist, we know that our yielding is not a sure consequence of the circumstances of trial in which we stand. Therefore the chain of uniformity does not bind volition. Catching at a quibble to hold him from being drawn into this concession, Mill might insist that his word is *could*, not *can* resist; and he might explain himself to mean that we could resist, if circumstances were different, but cannot as they are. But is consciousness of what we might help in another case, but cannot help in the present, a consciousness of not being here and now overpowered? If this is freedom, no man ever was a slave, for never was man placed in circumstances in which he could not have broken his bonds had not the said bonds been there and then too strong for him. In Mill's work *On Liberty* there is a chapter "Of Individuality as one of the conditions of well-being." In that enthusiastic and paradoxical vindication of individuality, one may mark the loathing with which the author turned from rigid necessarianism, a loathing which has got the better of his respect for consistency, and wrung from him a confession of free will in the midst of a treatise that argues universal uniformity.

VIII

"What experience makes known is the fact of an invariable sequence between every event and some special combination of antecedent conditions, in such sort that wherever and whenever that union of antecedents exists, the event does not fail to occur. Any *must* in the case, any necessity, other than the unconditional universality of the fact, we know nothing of. . . . The so-called Necessitarians . . . affirm, as a truth of experience, that volitions do, in point of fact, follow determinate moral antecedents with the same uniformity, and, when we have sufficient knowledge of the circumstances, with the same certainty as physical effects follow their physical causes. . . . This is what Necessitarians affirm, and they court every possible mode in which its truth can be verified. They test it by each person's observation of his own volitions. They test it by each person's observation of the voluntary actions of those with whom he comes into contact, and by the power which every one has of foreseeing actions with a degree of exactness proportioned to his previous experience and knowledge of the agents, and with a certainty often quite equal to that with which we predict the commonest physical events. They test it further by the statistical results of the observation of human beings acting in numbers sufficient to eliminate the influences which operate only on a few, and which on a large scale neutralise one another, leaving the total result about the same as if the volitions of the whole mass had been affected by such only of the determining causes as were common to them all. In cases of this description the results are as uniform, and may be as accurately foretold, as in any physical enquiries in which the effect depends upon a multiplicity of causes. The cases in which volitions seem too uncertain to be confidently predicted are those in which our knowledge of the influences antecedently in operation is so incomplete, that with equally imperfect data there would be the same uncertainty in the predictions of the astronomer and chemist. On these grounds it is con-

tended that our choice between the conflicting incon-
ceivables should be the same in the case of volitions
as of all other phenomena; we must reject equally in
both cases the hypothesis of spontaneousness, and consider them all as caused. A volition is a moral effect,
which follows the corresponding moral causes as certainly and invariably as physical effects follow their
physical causes. Whether it *must* be so, I acknowledge
myself to be entirely ignorant, be the phenomenon
moral or physical; and I condemn, accordingly, the
word Necessity as applied to either case. All I know is
that it always *does*."

This, and the following extracts, are from Mill's
Examination of Sir William Hamilton's Philosophy. Mill
here repeats what he has written in his *Logic*, that is
to say, he repeats Locke and Hume. I am, therefore,
compelled to repeat myself. I count it no disadvantage,
on a difficult topic, to be led into some repetition.

We have experience of necessity, and of what Mill
terms the "*a priori* must," quite as much as of invariable sequence and the "*a posteriori* does." Experience
is either immediate or mediate: it takes the form either
of intuition or inference. We cannot be always, nor
go everywhere; we cannot, therefore, gain immediate
experience of the working of a law in all times and
places. Creatures of a day, we cannot crowd an invariable sequence into our field of view. If we know any
such sequence, we know it only by inference, by assuming that an observed uniformity obtains beyond
the sphere of observation. But how justify this inference, how warrant the passage from "It does so far as
I have seen" to "It always does"? The *a posteriori*

"does" does very well; but the *a posteriori* "will do,"
I fear, will not do.

The *a priori* "must" comes to the rescue. If we
know what must be, we have ground to predict what
will be. How, then, do we know what must be? And,
first, how do we conceive it? By considering our in-
tuitions of what is. Surely we do right to examine
ideas which we have already got. We do no violence
to experience by counting the treasure which experience has bestowed on us. Intuition of self reveals "I
am," "I do," and thence "I can." The reverse of that
is "I cannot"; whence, by reduplication of the negative, "I cannot not," which is "I must." Transferring
the idea from self to not-self, we conceive "thou
must," "it must." But when do we know that a thing
must be? So far as we are concerned, that must be
which we find ourselves unable to prevent. To prevent a thing by our personal exertions we require to
know of it: ignorance in us means incapacity of interference. Given, therefore, an agent without understanding, we know that it cannot help whatever it does
or suffers; that it must do all that it can do, and suffer
all it can suffer under the circumstances in which it is
placed; that it is, in fact, a necessary agent. Whatever
it can do it does, and must do, if there be a term to
work upon within its sphere of action. What a brute
agent once does, it must ever do, *il ne sait pas faire au-
trement*. This necessity cleaves to the substantial abiding nature of a brute agent. To know that nature,
then, in the present, contains a knowledge of its action
in the future. A phenomenon of matter will be, because

it must be. That *positis ponendis* it must be we see in the cognition of the noumenon, the material substance which is at once the necessary agent, efficient cause of formerly observed phenomena, and the guarantee of like effects to follow under like conditions to come.

Rational natures often act unconsciously: they wake up to consciousness of mental states not of their own choosing. But then they can refrain from enhancing such a state within themselves: at the same time they can enhance it. The fuller their reflection, the greater their liberty in this particular. Looking into themselves, they become masters of their affections. Thus they are free to will or, as the Elizabethan writers said, to *affect*, or not to will and affect the objects that occur. But for this freedom, the verb *can* in our mouths would be foolish. "I can go to bed" means, in the first place, "I can make up my mind to do so." If my resolve were determined for me by the accidents of my position, it would be as idle for me, sitting in my chair, to say, "I can go to bed," as for the stones of Westminster Abbey, could they find a voice, to cry to the Dean and Chapter assembled below, "We can fall and crush you." Allow the possible as distinct from the actual, and one must allow the impossible, and thence the necessary and the contingent. To deny necessity is to deny possibility and impossibility. But it is as egregious wilfulness in a psychologist to set aside any element of human consciousness as for a chemist to expel from his laboratory chlorine and its compounds, forsooth because he has a theory with which those bodies do not square. As such a theory of chemistry

13

would be "done all on one side," so, too, is the philosophy one-sided that ignores necessity. And Mill does ignore necessity: he will not hear of it in physical science: he banishes it from the science of mind. Still the phrase, "It must be," has a meaning: every man understands it: a philosopher should take account of it.

Mill alleges three proofs, not of the necessary, but of the invariable sequence of volitions from certain antecedents. He appeals, first, to self-consciousness. Here is room not so much for controversy as for reflection. Reflection upon self is indispensable to the psychologist. It is, nevertheless, a somewhat untrustworthy source of knowledge. Entering into ourselves, we see what we go to see, and few of us go to see ourselves as we are. However, there is one reason for thinking that the insincerity in this question rests not with those psychologists who affirm the consciousness of free will. For what does that imply? "My will is free," in the mouth of a man on earth, implies, among other things, this: "I am capable of sinning." That, again, if we consider who the speaker is, further implies, to a greater or less extent, "I have sinned." Believers in free will believe in sin. One section, also, of disbelievers in free will have professed to believe in sin: I mean the Old Calvinists. The greater number, however, of disbelievers in free will, including all who deny the doctrine on other than theological grounds, have no belief in sin. They believe in noxious actions, restrainable by motives, but not in sinful actions. "Thou art the man" is not their word to the evil-

doer. They would shield him with Adam's excuses,—
his wife, the serpent, his temper and his circumstances.
They put crime in the same rank with disease: they
would have a criminal operated on for his cure; not
punished for his guilt. "Sweet shall be thy rest," says
the author of the *Imitation of Christ*, "sweet shall be thy
rest, if thy heart do not rebuke thee." The rest which
phenomenalists enjoy ought to be delicious indeed:
their heart cannot rebuke them, if they are, as they
represent themselves, unconscious as babes of the very
possibility of sinning. There is but one way heartily
to enjoy this world; that is, to put sin out of the list
of possibilities to be thought of. This comfortable way
phenomenalists have found. But the author quoted
above, speaking of ungodly men, who say they are at
peace, gives this warning, "Believe them not, for the
wrath of GOD shall rise of a sudden, and their deeds
shall be brought to nothing, and their speculations
shall perish." To deny sin is hardly the way to escape
the wrath to come, if it be to come. And men know
it is to come, and they know why, because in spite of
themselves they know that they have sinned. The
sense of sinfulness is written too deep in man's heart,
it has operated too widely amongst mankind, to be a
misconception, a psychological solecism. But it is no
more unless the will be free. Sin impossible? Would
it were so! But I fear that, were it not possible, men
could never have imagined such a horror. I conclude
that, of the philosophers who find free will in their
consciousness and sin upon their conscience, and of
those others who declare that they are unconscious

alike of being free and of having sinned, the latter are the more likely to be deceiving themselves, and to have not the truth in them.

Mill's second proof is borrowed from the fact that men can foretell each other's behaviour better or worse as they know more or less about one another. This fact proves nothing for him, if it stands as well with liberty as with uniformity in volition. And so it does. Free will is not indifference to motives: it is absence of any absolute constraint from the particular motive that is uppermost in the mind at any given moment. But there may be more or less an approach to constraint. A person is left more free under some motives than under others. A knowledge of his motives is a probable clue to his action. Still more is the probability of the estimate increased, if, along with motives, we know also his character, which we may know by knowing how he has behaved on similar occasions before. Every time a man does a thing, he diminishes his liberty of not doing it next time; he makes the act in some degree natural to him, and necessary in so far as it is natural. A habit is not broken without a special motive. The better a man's habits and motives are known, the more calculable his action becomes, calculable, I mean, with an ever increasing probability. Nor do I care to deny that some of man's actions may be calculated with absolute certainty. Such actions, if such there be, are necessary; but frequently they are what is called " free in their cause," being acts proceeding from a habit which was engendered originally of free acts. While Mill

holds that all acts are absolutely calculable in themselves, and are relatively incalculable to us because of
our ignorance of their antecedents, libertarians will
have it that some acts are absolutely beyond calculation, as not following rigidly from antecedents. Neither
view is inconsistent with the facts of our experience.
Necessarianism is not provable *a posteriori*.

Mill's third proof from "statistical results" shows
no more than this, that many men are sure to do what
all are inclined to do. Probability for each is certainty
for some, out of a large number, but not for any definite individuals. Free will, however, is an attribute of
men taken individually, not collectively. And antecedent probability of action is compatible with a degree
of freedom.

I reject, equally with Mill, "the hypothesis of spontaneousness" about volitions, and " I consider them
all as caused." That is to say, I do not believe an act
of the will to come out of nothing, a causeless phenomenon. I hold that the person who wills causes his
own volition, under certain motives as conditions. To
Mill the person is nobody; that is why he would call
a free act "spontaneous," meaning that it has no cause.
I do not, however, agree that volitions are "caused"
in Mill's sense of the term, or that an "explanation"
can be found for them, as for physical events.

"A volition," says Mill, "is a moral effect, which
follows the corresponding moral causes as certainly and
invariably as physical effects follow their causes." The
absurdity of this proposition is manifest, when we convert it into the following equivalent form: "A volition

is a conscious act, which is done by a conscious agent
or person, as necessarily as an unconscious act is done
by an unconscious agent or thing."

IX

"To be conscious of free will must mean, to be
conscious before I have decided that I am able to decide either way. Exception may be taken *in limine* to
the use of the word consciousness in such an application. Consciousness tells me what I do or feel. But
what I am *able* to do is not a subject of consciousness.
Consciousness is not prophetic; we are conscious of
what is, not of what will or can be. We never know
that we are able to do a thing, except from having done
it, or something equal and similar to it. We should
not know that we were capable of action at all, if we
had never acted. Having acted, we know, as far as that
experience reaches, how we are able to act; and this
knowledge, when it has become familiar, is often confounded with and called by the name of consciousness."

I do, *I can*, and *I am*, are three facets of the same
truth, all three known together in present consciousness. *I do* implies *I can*. *I do* and *I can* imply *I am*,
for there is no activity nor power in non-existence.
Again, *I am* signifies *I can* and also *I do;* there is no
substantial being without power, and there is no
power where there is no act, though outward action is
not coextensive with power. *I do* in the present, *I can*
in the present, and *I am* in the present. Mill acknowledges the present truth of *I do* and *I am*, but not of
I can. He thinks that when I declare *I can*, I announce
some future fact; but "consciousness," he says, "is
not prophetic." Conscious I am of being, Mill allows,

and conscious of doing, but not conscious of power.
My belief in any power of my own he holds to be an
inference from what I have done to what I shall do
again in like circumstances. But surely, "I can do a
thing" does not mean "I shall do it." When I act, I
am conscious alike of action and of power, both in
the present. The action passes, but the consciousness
of power remains. There is nothing "prophetic" about
it. It is true that we learn our powers by exercising
them. And we learn that we have a free will by exercising it. It is a consciousness that comes of experience. There is no innate idea of free will. The will
is not free in childhood. To say that a child has come
to the use of reason means that his will is now beginning to assume command of his conduct. We learn
to will as we learn to lift. There are weights that we
cannot so much as stir. And about many circumstances
and conditions of life our will is utterly powerless. We
learn to know hard necessity, things that we cannot
help, in contrast with what we can help. Necessity
strikes us most when it is about feelings of our own,
of a pleasurable or painful kind. Many such feelings,
e.g., those of temperature in our own bodies, are partly
under our control and partly beyond our control.
Such experience especially helps on the cognition of
free will. But free will comes out most of all in the
matter of impulses. Moral education begins in the
checking of impulses, notably those passionate out-
bursts of crying characteristic of infants generally. Aided
by much persuasive impulse from without, the child
comes to cry a little less. There is nothing of free will

here, because there is not as yet any reflex consciousness, nothing more than that formative process which
we observe in the higher animals under the training
of man. The assertion of self against impulse is very
gradual. When that assertion takes definite shape, free
will has begun. One day an impulse is curbed in this
way; another day it is allowed free scope. But in
giving it scope, the young agent remembers, "I helped
crying, or getting angry, or frightened, yesterday."
The inference thence is not beyond the range of a
child of six or seven, "I might have helped getting
angry to-day." There we have an initial consciousness
of free will. There is nothing mysterious in the process, nothing inconsistent with the nature of a conscious act. It is a reading of one's own present state
in the light of a remembered similar past. There is
no reference at all to the future; nothing of the element that Mill calls "prophetic."

Mill's mistake, common to him with Locke, is that
of confusing the will to act in a certain way with the
power of executing such volition. Nothing certainly
is more frequent than for people to fancy themselves
conscious of abilities, which further experience proves
that they do not possess. Conscious of his swimming
powers, so he thinks, the unfortunate youth jumps
into the quarry pond and is drowned. We have
in such cases to distinguish between man and his circumstances. Man is conscious of what depends on
himself; he is not conscious of what depends on circumstances. He makes an effort and hopes it will suc-
ceed. The effort is perhaps the main element of success,

but it is not success. To be conscious of ability is to be conscious of that which in us lies, not of what lies without us. Therefore, 'I am conscious I can swim,' is a twofold judgement of consciousness and of inference. It comes to this: 'I am conscious I can try, and I argue from past experience that my attempt will be successful.' The consciousness here is infallible, but further experience in unwonted circumstances may overthrow the inference. Hence we may learn to distinguish what truth there is in Mill's saying, that the assertion *I can* is "prophetic." So far as it means, 'I can use my endeavours,' the assertion *I can* is a fact of present consciousness: so far as it means, 'those endeavours will be adequate to the occasion,' it is an inference from the past to the future.

X

"But this conviction, whether termed consciousness or only belief, that our will is free—what is it? Of what are we convinced? I am told that whether I decide to do or to abstain, I feel that I could have decided the other way. I ask my consciousness what I do feel, and I find, indeed, that I feel (or am convinced) that I could have chosen the other course if I had preferred it; but not that I could have chosen one course while I preferred another. When I say preferred, I, of course, include with the thing itself, all that accompanies it. . . Take any alternative: say to murder or not to murder. I am told that if I elect to murder, I am conscious that I could have elected to abstain: but am I conscious that I could have abstained if my aversion to the crime, and my dread of its consequences, had been weaker than the temptation? If

I elect to abstain, in what sense am I conscious that I could have elected to commit the crime ? Only if I had desired to commit it with a desire stronger than my horror of murder; not with one less strong. When we think of ourselves hypothetically as having acted otherwise than we did, we always suppose a difference in the antecedents : we picture ourselves as having known something that we did not know, or not known something that we did know; which is a difference in the external motives; or as having desired something or disliked something more or less than we did; which is a difference in the internal motives. I, therefore, dispute altogether that we are conscious of being able to act in opposition to the strongest present desire or aversion."

Let us for a moment suppose that the doctrine, here laid down by Mill, is true. Let us take his example of a man who has before him an alternative to murder or not to murder. Then, if that man's aversion to the crime and his dread of its consequences are weaker than the temptation, he cannot abstain from the murder: he needs must commit it in that case. If, on the other hand, his desire to commit the crime is weaker than his horror of it, he cannot commit the murder, but must needs abstain from it. Whence I argue thus. Either the temptation is stronger than the horror of the crime, or the horror of the crime is stronger than the temptation,—the case of the two being equal is a blank. Which ever way it is, the man's election is necessitated; and as of this, so of every other election that a man may be called upon to make, all are necessitated; therefore, the true theory of volition, as Mill expounds it, is absolute necessarianism.

Having followed Mill to a goal which he himself somewhat deprecates, let us retrace our steps to the point where we differ from him. It is a slight point, so slight that he has overlooked its being a possible occasion of difference. He " disputes altogether that we are conscious of being able to act in opposition to the strongest present desire or aversion." I dispute it also; indeed, in strict parlance, though, of course, not in the popular sense, I deny it. We cannot act in opposition to the strongest present desire, while that desire is at the present strongest. But frequently we are able to refrain from acting in accordance with the strongest present desire (or aversion). Suppose I have a desire to pull a house down because it is inconvenient, and also a desire to leave it standing because it is endeared to me by old associations. I cannot feel two such incompatible desires both at exactly the same instant, but I feel now one and now the other. Each in turn is the stronger at the instant at which I feel it, though one may be stronger than the other on the whole, as coming oftener and being more intense when it does come. If the proposition, which Mill and I alike dispute, simply means that I can finally act against the desire which on the whole is stronger, I cannot stand with Mill, for the proposition in that sense is true. But if the meaning is that I can do the very reverse of what at the moment of my action I supremely long to do, I protest with Mill against the proposition. To me, as to Mill, it appears incredible that a man should choose one course, and at the same time prefer, altogether prefer, the reverse. Such a choice would turn the laws of volition topsy-turvy. Let us go back to the example of the house. At this instant, we will say, the desire of pulling down the building is uppermost in my soul. By the very fact that I have that desire now, I do not desire at the same moment to let the building stand. I have a spontaneous complacency in the idea of destruction; and that, while it lasts, prevents me from being complacent in the idea of conservation.* If I consummate any volition now by a reflex approval of a spontaneous complacency, the approval must fall on the complacency which I have now. I cannot at present make up my mind to keep the house standing: for the one "bill," so to speak, at present awaiting my royal assent is a bill to pull it down. A man cannot will in opposition to, I do not say his animal or physical, but his psychical and volitional impulse while that impulse actually reigns; nor being spontaneously complacent in one purpose can he become then and there reflexly complacent in another. Thus far I go along with Mill. He proceeds tacitly to assume that a man must positively act and reflexly will in accordance with his strongest present desire, and there I fall off from him. I say the man can wait. Once more to the house. Desiring to pull the old place down I cannot resolve to keep it standing, but I can stay and view my desire. And while I view it, the desire fades away, and I remain thinking, but not willing, what I shall do with the old place. The desire to keep it now rises and becomes predominant. I cannot will to pull the building

---

*The coiner's press must stamp just that bit of metal which at that moment lies under it, if at that moment it stamps anything at all.

down while I feel an actual desire to keep it; but at the same time I need not will to keep it. So I go on till at last I will in accordance with some present desire.

When the volition is completed, I look back upon my act. I say it was freely done, by which I mean, not that I could at the instant have acted otherwise, but that I could at the instant have refrained from acting in the way I did. In the moment when the act of my will was done, though I could not have acted otherwise, I need not have acted at all. I might have been quiescent: I might simply not have approved the complacency at that time being. Without any difference in the antecedents, without any learning of anything that I did not know, or becoming ignorant of aught that I did know, or desiring or disliking more or less than I spontaneously did desire or dislike, I might have held aloof from that complacency which I sanctioned and made into a full volition. But for me then to have embraced a different complacency, and to have performed a different act of the will, does suppose a difference in the antecedents, just such a difference as Mill says "we always suppose when we think of ourselves hypothetically as having acted otherwise than we did." Mill's dictum is right, formally for the psychological instant of decision, but not for the whole of the deliberative process which is popularly called the "action."*

* See Locke, n. 9.

XI

"It is not the belief that we shall be made account-able, which can be deemed to require or presuppose the free-will hypothesis; it is the belief that we ought so to be; that we are justly accountable; that guilt deserves punishment. It is here that the main issue is joined between the two opinions. In discussing it, there is no need to postulate any theory respecting the nature or criterion of moral distinctions. It matters not for this purpose whether the right and wrong of actions de-pends on the consequences they tend to produce or on an inherent quality of the actions themselves. It is indifferent whether we are utilitarians or anti-utilitarians; whether our ethics rest on intuition or on experience. It is sufficient if we believe that there is a difference between right and wrong, and a natural reason for preferring the former. . . The real question is one of justice—the legitimacy of retribution or punishment. On the theory of necessity, we are told, man cannot help acting as he does, and it cannot be just that he should be punished for what he cannot help. Not if the expectation of punishment enables him to help it, and is the only means by which he can be enabled to help it? . . . There are two ends which on the necessitarian theory are sufficient to justify punishment: the benefit of the offender himself and the protection of others. The first justifies it, because to benefit a person cannot be to do him an injury. To punish him for his own good, provided the inflictor has any proper title to constitute himself a judge, is no more unjust than to administer medicine. . . In its other aspect punishment is a precaution taken by society in self-defence. . . If it is possible to have just rights, it cannot be unjust to defend them. Free will or no free will, it is just to punish so far as is necessary for this purpose, exactly as it is just to put a wild beast to death, without unnecessary suffering, for the same object. Now, the primitive consciousness we are said to have, that we are accountable for our actions, and that, if we violate the rule of right, we shall deserve punishment, I contend is nothing else than our knowledge that punishment will be just; that by such conduct we shall place ourselves in the position in which our fellow-creatures, or the Deity, or both, will naturally and may justly inflict punishment upon us. By using the word *justly* I am not assuming in the explanation the thing I profess to explain. As before observed, I am entitled to postulate the reality and the knowledge and feeling of moral distinctions."

Mill is fighting against an objection which may be put into syllogism thus.

We cannot know that we ought to be punished for our misdeeds, without knowing also that our wills are free.

But we do know that we ought to be punished for our misdeeds.

Therefore we know also that our wills are free.

Mill denies the major of this syllogism, and undertakes to prove the contradictory, that we can know that we ought to be punished for our misdeeds, without knowing also that our wills are free; in other words, that the notion of just punishment does not involve the notion of free will. The way to prove this thesis would be to explain the meaning of the phrase, "we ought to be punished," and to show, if possible, that the phrase does not contain any reference to free will. But Mill starts with the surprising announcement that the reason of the right and wrong of actions, which explains

why we ought to be punished when we do wrong,
matters not for the purpose of his proof. Surely, it is
on that very reason that the proof depends. How can
anyone discuss why punishment is just, without his
argument involving some view as to the essential
nature of justice? But that again involves some theory
of morals. Indeed, one of the greatest treatises on the
theory of morals ever written, the *Republic* of Plato,
starts from this very inquiry, What is justice? Mill's
antagonists here contend that the denial of free will
puts quite a new face on justice and just punishment;
and that the ordinary notion of justice and just punishment is founded on the assumption of free will; that
consequently, to ordinary minds, to punish a man for
a deed which there and then he could not help is
unjust. Mill's reply, fair enough in its way, is that the
ordinary notion of justice is altogether a mistake. He
proceeds to inculcate instead his own notion of justice
and just punishment, which is the blankest utilitarianism. Mill's compeer, Bain, correctly writes: "Assuming that the imposition of punishment is the distinc-
tive property of acts held to be morally wrong, we are
next to inquire on what grounds such acts are forbidden
and hindered by all the force that society or individuals
possess. What are the reasons or considerations re-
quiring each one to abstain from the performance of
certain actions, and to concur in a common prohibition
of them, enforced by stringent penalties? The answer
to this is the theory of morals."* This is saying, and it
is well said, that some theory of morals is implied in the
belief that certain actions ought to be punished. How

* *Emotions and Will*, second edition, p. 254.

then can Mill pretend that "it is indifferent whether we are utilitarians or anti-utilitarians?" His whole argument is constructed on a basis of utilitarianism.

When a philosopher writes, "There is no need to postulate," let the reader beware, and till he sees it to be otherwise, let him expect that his author is going to take for granted the point which he says there is no need to postulate. It is not dishonesty on the philosopher's part that prompts him to this stretch of the "privy paw." The stealth is ascribable to a mixture of zeal and mistrust. Observing some pet doctrine in want of a particular support, and doubting of our ability to secure it in face of the opposition of our adversary, we yield to the nervous eagerness of desire which makes men say the reverse of what they should say, and we bid the other party distinctly to take notice how we scorn that support on which all the while our doctrine rests. Thus Mill needs the utilitarian morality to bear out his assertion, that crime ought to be punished, free will or no free will. But his opponents are not utilitarians, and to convert them is not worth his while to try. Therefore he denies his need, at the same time taking what he needs for granted. He lays down utilitarian definitions concerning crime and punishment and justice. He lays beside them the necessarian principle, that a man cannot help the crime that he commits. He applies the said definitions to the said principle, and the result appears accordingly, that it is just to punish a man for the crime that he cannot help. In other words, it is expedient for the greatest happiness of the greatest number, that a man who has been com-

14

pelled to mar that happiness for want of a motive to maintain it, should suffer such an amount of pain as shall furnish a motive to compel him on the next temptation to respect the common interests of humanity. A just procedure, on condition that crime be made out an accident, punishment a surgical operation, justice expediency, and man a motive-worked automaton. At that rate I readily understand how, " free will or no free will, it is just to punish so far as is necessary for this purpose, exactly as it is just to put a wild beast to death."

Utilitarianism is a ruthlessly logical system, but it is not a system of morals. Elsewhere I have styled it " an abyss of chaos and confusion," in which " moral philosophy finds her grave."* Abiding by that verdict, I say that to punish a man for what he cannot help is an insult to the dignity and a violation of the rights of man. To punish is not simply to pain: it is to pain and to blame together. Though it be sometimes just, for a man's own benefit and for the protection of others, to make him suffer pain for what he cannot help, it can never be just to blame him for what he cannot help. The castigations which we inflict on children and brute animals are only styled punishments in an improper sense of the term, inasmuch as they are not accompanied with moral reproach. It is from an exclusive study of this improper sense that utilitarians have evolved their theory of punishment, a theory which supposes that a wicked man, a " naughty boy," and a

* Ethics and Natural Law, Stonyhurst Series, pp. 177-189.

restive horse, are all on a level as objects of punishment.
A moment's consideration destroys this supposition.
Man, boy, and horse receive stripes alike; but the man
is blamed severely, the boy perhaps slightly, the horse
not at all. The blame is an essential portion of the man's
punishment; it is that which gives it the sting. The
animosity shown against men of blood, marking them
off from mere beasts of prey, Mill would set down to
the desire to see an example made of noxious men, lest
they should breed imitators. That is indeed a reason why
the murderer should suffer. But it is not a reason for
holding him in abomination. Abomination is not prospective, precautionary, prudential, as Mill would
have the entire treatment of wrong-doers to be. To
punish is not to dispense suffering as a chemist dispen-
ses drugs: punishment is suffering attended with blame.
Blame supposes that the delinquent could and ought
to have done otherwise.

As there seems to be something incompatible with
utilitarian ideas in the reprobation heaped on crime
by the common people, it will be desirable in the day
when criminals shall be confined among the beasts, for
some disciple of Mill to stand beside the cages to
rectify the vulgar errors of the visitors. The tenor of
his lecture might be as follows:

"That bear there you observe, ladies and gentlemen, yesterday morning hugged his keeper: the man
was carried out dead from that fatal embrace. The
animal in the next compartment is a man, who has
murdered his wife. As the other bears are not likely

to be influenced by that one bear's example, it has not been thought necessary to punish him: but the new keeper has received instructions not to take liberties with his charge. The man, however, is to be made a warning to his fellows. It were in evil precedent for our species if a husband could kill his wife with impunity. Therefore is he deprived of his liberty, and any afternoon at one o'clock you may see him publicly flogged. Not that his guilt is greater than the bear's: but prudence requires that he should undergo a more exemplary punishment. Be pleased, therefore, not to censure, blame, loathe or abominate the man any more than you loathe the brute. You call the murderer a brute, and it is well you should: only remember that nature made him what he is, no less inevitably than she made the bear. The keeper's death took place in accordance with an invariable law. Had he indeed not enraged the animal, the law would not have come into operation. But he did enrage the animal, and the animal killed him necessarily. You do not blame Bruin for that. The man is as blameless as the bear. He had from nature, to start with, a certain organisation and certain susceptibilities of character. He grew up in the midst of circumstances, which followed other circumstances in unvarying sequence, like the heat and cold, and sun and rain, under which a water-lily springs on the bosom of a lonely lake. A plant's growth is determined by two factors, germinal capacity and environment: so is a man's character made for him by nature and by circumstances. This poor fellow could not help killing his wife. There are motives which would have saved him from the crime, but they were out of his reach. He had them not, and could not get them. If his wife had been wearing an iron helmet, the blow would not have proved fatal. But she had no helmet to wear, and so was fain to die, as her husband was fain to kill. One is no more to be blamed than the other for what neither could help. It was the uniformity of nature, the same which tempers the heat of the sun and measures the orbit of the moon, that brought the husband to strike with the cleaver and the wife to die of the wound. Let us hope, ladies and gentlemen, that nature is not steadily preparing, in the order of her sure sequences, a similar fate for you and me."

This, it will be said, is turning philosophy into buffoonery. It may be buffoonery, but, to the writer at least, it is not mirth. It saddens my heart to read utterances like the following: "You discern nothing while your eye is fixed on Archelaus himself. . . But when you turn to the persons whom he has killed, banished, or ruined . . . there is no lack of argument to justify that sentiment which prompts a reflecting spectator to brand him as a disgraceful man. . . It will indeed be at once seen that the taint or distemper with which Archelaus is supposed to inoculate himself when he commits signal crime . . . is a pure fancy or poetical metaphor on the side of Plato himself."* To say that sin is no stain is to say that it is not sin. A criminal

---

* Grote's *Plato,* II, 109, 111. There is nothing "disgraceful" in being a usurper and a tyrant, if one cannot help it. Men should not be reproached for their natural defects nor for the circumstances of their education.

in this view is toned down to a hurtful agent: "a Borgia and a Catiline" appear no worse than "storms and earthquakes." Wicked men certainly are influenced by motives, hurricanes are not. The inference which I should draw, as an utilitarian, measuring moral evil by material damages, is that hurricanes are more wicked than men, as being more incorrigibly noxious. A deed of ours which we cannot help may hurt our fellow-men, but we are quite aware that that is no sin. We should not resent being put to inconvenience to prevent the recurrence of the mishap,—being shut up by ourselves, for instance, when we have unwittingly communicated an infection. But we should resent being punished for it, that is, being reproached as well as inconvenienced. It is the earliest excuse of a child, 'I could not help it.' The stupid, rude answer, 'But I'll make you help it,' has a ring of tyranny and injustice in the ear of a little one.

One last word on the theory of punishment. The theory, as we have seen, needs to be modified to fit in with the hypothesis of determinism. But, I observe, not only does the theory, as a theme of academic discussion, need modification: an important change must likewise be made in our criminal jurisprudence, and in the practice of our courts of justice, those arbiters of life and death. I refer to the case of the criminal lunatic, afflicted with homicidal mania. Like other madmen, these unhappy persons are by no means inaccessible to motives, especially of the more violent sort. It is quite possible to inspire them with fear and so deter them from offending; and this possibility is greater, and the deterrent more effectual, ere they have yet shed blood. These early stages of the malady should be contemplated by the preventive eye of the judge. If a new legal maxim were introduced, and enforced by example before the eyes of all men, that insanity shall no longer enter into the verdict, and that criminal lunatics henceforth shall be hung for homicide as inexorably as other murderers are hung, then persons of unsettled reason, and others whose criminal habits are gradually unsettling their reason, would have a strong motive provided them to keep them from shedding blood, and this provision would be a notable addition to the safety of the community. Why should not the law provide this additional security? If any criminal at all should be hung for murder on determinist principles, we should hang the criminal lunatic for murder. Of all dangerous persons he is the most dangerous: his type is the most clearly marked: his character is the most set, and his execution would be the most exemplary.

The sole reason for sparing the life of this dangerous person is drawn from the ancient belief of that Christianity in which European States were conceived and nurtured, the belief that, not being a free agent, the lunatic is not responsible for his deed; that with his character and under his circumstances he could not help it; that, therefore, he has not sinned before GOD, and, consequently, should not be visited with extreme punishment by man.* Civilly noxious, and, therefore,

---

* " Never by human judgement ought a man to be punished with the pain of the lash (*pœna flagelli*), so as to be put to death, or

'o be kept in confinement, he is still morally innocent, and retains the right of a man to live, a right
which no man forfeits except voluntarily and freely,
by choosing to behave like a wild beast.* This poor
lunatic still claims the benefit of the medieval axiom:
" The life of the just makes for the preservation and
promotion of the good of the community; and, therefore, it is nowise lawful to slay the innocent."†

But all these considerations of the old libertarianism
are swept away by modern determinism, as ruthlessly
as they were abolished by Hobbes. To any determinist,
or necessarian, a punishable murderer is not one who,
being what he was by nature and character, and tempted
as he found himself, could possibly have acted otherwise than as he did act to the slaying of his fellowman: he is simply a highly noxious element of society,
whose extirpation will be a good riddance, and will act
as a motive to deter similar characters from imitating
his conduct. If the determinist judge will hang any
man, let him hang this criminal lunatic.

XII

" If any one thinks that there is justice in the
infliction of purposeless suffering, that there is a natural affinity between the two ideas of guilt and punish-

maimed, or beaten with [grievous] stripes, without his own fault.
But with the pain of loss (*pœna damni*) one is punished even in
human judgement without fault, but not without cause."—Aquinas, *Sum. Theol.* 2a 2æ, q. cviii, art. 4 ad 2.

* I beseech the reader to whom these ideas are strange to study
them in St Thomas, *Sum. Theol.* 2a 2æ, q. lxiv, articles 1, 2, 3, 6;
they may be read in English in *Aquinas Ethicus*, ii, pp. 39-42, 46;
cf. *Ethics and Natural Law*, pp. 203, 349, 350.

† St Thomas, l.c.

ment, which makes it intrinsically fitting that wherever there has been guilt, pain should be inflicted by way of retribution, I acknowledge that I can find no argument to justify punishment inflicted on this principle. As a legitimate satisfaction to feelings of indignation and resentment which are on the whole salutary and worthy of cultivation, I can in certain cases admit it; but here it is still a means to an end. The merely retributive view of punishment derives no justification from the doctrine I support. But it derives quite as little from the free-will doctrine. Suppose it true that the will of a malefactor, when he committed an offence, was free, or, in other words, that he acted badly, not because he was of a bad disposition, but for no reason in particular, it is not easy to deduce from this the conclusion that it is just to punish him. That his acts were beyond the command of motives might be a good reason for keeping out of his way, or placing him under bodily restraint; but no reason for inflicting pain upon him, when that pain, by supposition, could not operate as a deterring motive. While the doctrine I advocate does not support the idea that punishment in mere retaliation is justifiable, it at the same time fully accounts for the general and natural sentiment of its being so. From our earliest childhood the ideas of doing wrong and of punishment are presented to our mind together, and the intense character of the impressions causes the association between them to attain the highest degree of closeness and intimacy. Is it strange, or unlike the usual processes of the human mind, that in these circumstances we should retain the feeling, and forget the reason on which it is grounded? But why do I speak of forgetting? In most cases the reason has never in our early education been presented to the mind. The only ideas presented have been those

of wrong and punishment, and an inseparable association has been created between these directly, without
the help of any intervening idea. This is quite enough
to make the spontaneous feelings of mankind regard
punishment and a wrong-doer as naturally fitted to
each other—as a conjunction appropriate in itself, in-
dependently of any consequences."

There is no strategic advantage in marching in force
upon a position entirely removed from the seat of war.
" He acted badly for no reason in particular " is such
an irrelevant position in the present controversy: no
necessarian need attack what no libertarian holds. Of
course the malefactor acts for some reason and some
motive: of course certain reasons and motives appeal
strongly to his peculiar disposition. But every true
human act, though necessarily done on some motive,
is not done according to one motive rather than
according to another except under the conscious
superintendence and final arbitrement of the presiding
Ego. Whichever way the arbitrement goes, it goes
upon " some reason in particular ": the crux of the
question is, Why upon this reason rather than upon
that ? Libertarians assert that no "why" of physical
determination, like the " whys " of physical science,
is assignable ; and that, therefore, "moral" science is
not, what necessarians make it, a "physical" science.
For my own part I should keep out of the way of a
man to whom it was the same thing to have a motive,
supervening upon a particular disposition, and to act
accordingly. Such is the behaviour of somnambulists, of
patients in delirium and of lunatics generally, but not

of men in their right senses. A man in his right senses, that is to say, a free agent, is one whose acts are not beyond the command of motives, nor yet wholly within the command of motives. Give a person a motive, and you incline him to act; you do not compel him. Motives, therefore, are useful means to employ, though they do not quite act like weights in a scale. It is advisable to lead your horse to the water, even though you cannot make him drink. He certainly will not drink unless he comes to water. And thus much of deterrent punishment on the theory of free will.

Now for free will and retributive punishment. An evil deed freely done calls for retribution. Not only should repetition be guarded against in the future, but the past wrong should be revenged. There should be " sorrow dogging sin." This is the keynote of tragedy, to which the human heart has responded sympathetically in all ages.

Δράσαντα παθεῖν,
τριγέρων μῦθος τάδε φωνεῖ.*

What is it that a man does when he commits a crime? He does damage, and he does wrong: his act is evil physically and morally. The damage is to be repaired and hindered from recurring, like any other damage. If it is a wound inflicted, we send the patient to the hospital, and lay restraints upon the hasty temper and violent hand of the striker. Thus the physical evil is corrected. But the offending person has not only done damage, a stone may do that: he has, moreover, willed

* Æschylus, *Choephori,* 314.

to do damage, freely and wantonly. He himself personally was the main author of the mischief, not his motives. Without motives he could not have done evil: but the motives that he had were void of effect without his sanction. Not only, therefore, shall we labour to readjust his motives; we shall also blame him for having yielded to his motives as they stood, and blaming him we shall avenge the majesty of the moral law upon him, making him suffer for the wrong that he has freely done.

Man starts life with much good about him, the gift of nature and of GOD. He has as a duty of serving the Giver by keeping the law of nature; and that law he will discern in various measures according to circumstances of age, place and race. He can and he ought to help himself by the aid of his liberty to keep the law, as he understands it, and as the observance of it lies within his power. If he wilfully breaks the law,—not as it binds me, and as it would be atrocious for me to break it,—but as it binds *him*, and with a disobedience atrocious *even in him*, then he has entered upon a quarrel with his Maker, in which he, the man, is the aggressor. God essentially loves Himself and hates whatever is opposed to Him. He cannot be opposed but by a free agent. Ill will alone can set up against the Almighty; and an ill will is the single object of His hate. GOD, we are told, is love. The earth and the fullness thereof is the monument which GOD's love has built. But if His love is so efficacious, His hatred is not feeble. St Ignatius in his *Spiritual Exercises*, in the first Exercise on sin, puts before us the case of a man,

no matter who, "who for one mortal sin has gone to
hell ": he bids us ponder " how in sinning and acting
against Infinite Goodness such a one has been justly
damned for ever." Eternal punishment is the consummation of retributive justice, a consummation to over-
awe, but not to astonish us. We are not to be surprised at wilful, flagrant opposition to the Supreme
Goodness having its issue in endless evil. Holiness
and happiness are in GOD. It is not unnatural that
he who cuts himself off from holiness, should be cut
off from happiness; and that impiety, if not accompanied with misery, should at any rate end in misery.
Whoever renounces the law cannot expect to retain
the joy of the LORD. Whoever will not share GOD's
holiness, shall not share His happiness. We say commonly that man sins and GOD punishes. We might put
it otherwise that man, so far as in him lies, casts off
GOD, and then finds himself forlorn. Punishment is
not so much the remedy as the result of sin. When
GOD leaves things to take their course, the sinner is
chastised: mercy is more of a divine interference than
justice. When the angels sinned, we are told, " their
place was no more found in heaven."* Heaven had
become for them a foreign country, a climate in which
they could not thrive, and they fell down as dead
leaves drop from the trees in autumn.

The separation of the wicked from GOD, and their
consequent destruction, are thus pictured by Plato:

GOD, as the old tradition declares, holding in His hand
the beginning, middle and end of all that is, moves according

* Apocalypse xii, 8.

to His nature in a straight line towards the accomplishment
of His end. Justice always follows Him, and is the punisher
of those who fall short of the divine law. To that law he
who would be happy holds fast and follows it in all humility and order; but he who is lifted up with pride, or
money, or honour, or beauty, who has a soul hot with
folly and youth and insolence, and thinks that he has no
need of a guide or ruler, but is able himself to be the guide
of others, he, I say, is left deserted of GOD, καταλείπεται ἔρημος
θεοῦ; and being thus deserted he takes to him therso who
are like himself, and dances about in wild confusion, and many
think that he is a great man, but in a short time he pays a
penalty which justice cannot but approve, and is utterly de-
stroyed.*

Mill and his school enter vigorous protests against
any introduction of theology into philosophy. But
natural theology is a part of philosophy, the end and
crown of the science. To treat of crime and of punishment, without reference to the Supreme Ruler and
Judge of all the earth, is impossible to a serious
theist.

Having spoken of chastisements immediately divine,
I pass to those inflicted by civil society. Is it right for
civil society to punish one of its members merely with
a view to satisfaction for a past offence, without hope
either of the reformation of the culprit or the protection of society? It is not right, as I will show with all
possible brevity. To punish, one must have authority
over the delinquent. Against an equal there exists the
right of self-defence but not of punishment. The
awarding of punishments is a function of distributive
ustice, the actual exercise of which justice belongs to

*Laws, 716, Jowett's translation.

rulers, not to subjects.* The civil ruler must not punish beyond the measure of his authority. That measure is determined by the end of civil government, which end is the temporal happiness of the civil community, that the citizens may live together in peace and justice, with a sufficiency of wordly goods, and with so much of moral probity as is requisite for the outward good order and happiness of the State.† The civil magistrate cannot punish, *motu proprio*, except for this end. To the extent to which this end may reasonably be expected to be furthered, to that extent, and not beyond, may pains and penalties be imposed by the civil power.

But, though the State should not punish any man further than there is a prospect of good to mankind, yet the punishment inflicted under this limitation is retributive as well as corrective. A murderer should not be hung, except where the hanging is likely to hinder bloodshed; but when he his hung in that likelihood, men may well rejoice that he has got his deserts. We may rejoice to see sin expiated by suffering, though we should not inflict suffering on another person without his consent, solely for the expiation of his sins. We blame sin wherever we discover it. But, in order to award pain as well as blame, that is, to award punishment to a sinner, the civil magistrate should have some prospect of amending the offender or protecting society against him and his example. A wicked man deserves punishment, but his fellow-men

* St Thomas Aquinas, *Summa*, 2a, 2æ, q. lxi, art. 1 ad 3.
† Suarez, *De Legibus*, l. iii, c. 11, n. 7.

are not always the persons to punish him. Where they have the right to inflict punishment for their own purposes, they become, at the same time, the ministers of the vengeance of the LORD, and should consider themselves as such.

Mill draws an argument from "the punishment of crimes committed in obedience to a perverted conscience." He alludes by name to Ravaillac and Balthasar Gérard. Men like these, he thinks, are justly immolated to political expediency, without any regard to the "state of mind of the offender, further than as this may affect the efficacy of punishment as a means to its end." I observe that laws are made to deal with facts as they ordinarily occur. If a criminal's conscience has been perverted, it is commonly his own fault. The law, therefore, will not admit the plea of perversion of conscience. It supposes guilt in the man who, being of sound mind, does a criminal act.

These, then, are the positions which I advance against Mill. (1) It is unjust to punish a man, blame and distress him, for a deed which he could not help. (2) Even for deeds that he could help, the civil power should never punish a man further than the good of society requires; but within that limit he should be punished as well as in retribution for the past as in precaution against the future. (3) GOD does justly punish in certain cases by way of mere retaliation for the wrong done to His Divine Majesty.

One word in conclusion on the educational bearing of this discussion, as our pedagogists now insist on psychology for teachers. Let free will be an article of the teacher's psychological creed, if not on the higher ground of truth, then on the lower ground of utilitarian and pragmatic expediency. Where free will is denied, punish as we may, the training of the young in virtue will prove no easy task. When a child is punished, unless he confess at heart that he deserves it for his own waywardness and wilfulness, the punishment will not appear to him in any moral light but as a mere odious infliction. If there is no self-reproach, no iteration of the rod will ever lead a delinquent to think that wrong-doing is wrong and ought to be punished. His thought will be that, unfortunately, it is hard to do forbidden things and escape scot-free,—a widely different conclusion. But self-reproach brings in the consciousness of free will: we do not reproach ourselves for what we think we could not help. Evil, inevitable under the circumstances, is a matter of pure compassion.

XIII

"Suppose that there were two peculiar breeds of human beings,—one of them so constituted from the beginning that, however educated or treated, nothing could prevent them from always feeling and acting so as to be a blessing to all whom they approached; another, of such original perversity of nature that neither education nor punishment could inspire them with a feeling of duty, or prevent them from being active in evil-doing. Neither of these races of human beings would have free will; yet the former would be honoured as demigods, while the latter would be regarded and treated as noxious beasts: not punished perhaps, since punishment would have no effect upon them, and it might be thought wrong to indulge the mere instinct of vengeance: but kept carefully at a distance, and killed like other dangerous creatures when there was no other convenient way of being rid of them. We thus see that even under the utmost possible exaggeration of the doctrine of necessity the distinction between moral good and evil in conduct would not only subsist, but would stand out in a more marked manner than now, when the good and the wicked, however unlike, are still regarded as of one common nature."

If we consider a man's act apart from the manner in which it is elicited,—in other words, if we abstract from free will and determinism, neither affirming nor denying either,—no doubt a distinction between good and evil actions might still be kept up. Nay, even under the denial of free will, the action which we now know as good remains good, and the action which we know as evil remains evil. But under such denial we should regard the doers of such actions in quite a different light from that in which we view good men and bad men now. On this point I have written elsewhere:

And first of what remains of our present moral system, when it comes to be worked on determinist principles. The Ten Commandments remain unchanged. The list of vices and virtues remains unchanged. The ethical motives for virtue and against vice remain unchanged. The State continues to frame laws, commanding and forbidding the same things as before. The same conduct is praised and rewarded, or blamed and punished, as before, albeit not quite with the same intention. The portraits of the good man and of the bad man respectively have lost none of their external lineaments. The one is still self-controlled and self-denying, brave, loving, magnanimous and just. The other remains a sensualist, cruel and cowardly, frivolous, idle, heartless and untrustworthy. Nero is still bad, and Paul good. The exigencies of human nature and of human society have not lost their value. The good and happiness of the individual, and the prosperity of the society to which he belongs, require of him the same conduct as before. Goodness has not become less profitable, nor wickedness less detrimental and deplorable, now that both are recognised necessities. Wickedness is what it was in every respect save one; and the same deeds are wicked that were wicked. Goodness has lost only one of its attributes. Formerly the good man did what it befitted a man to do, having at the same time in the very act and circumstances of his well-doing the power to swerve from goodness: still he does the same things, but further it is to be noted that, with his character and circumstances, he cannot help doing them. And conversely of the wicked man, who is rightly enough pronounced by the determinist a dangerous, disgusting and offensive animal. Ugly conduct fits in with the determinist hypothesis as well as ugly architecture. We praise a flower, or a gun, or the "points" of a horse. There would be no difficulty in praising in that way a man in whose conduct we recognised no free will. Still he might be to us a grand fellow, a very useful creature. We might further encourage him with prospective praise, as an inducement to serve us still better, much in the same way that a driver pats his horse and utters kind cries to it on a hard road. Such praise, however, and the corresponding blame, cannot be called *moral approbation* and *reprobation*.*

There are two cases conceivable in which no education nor treatment could prevent a human being from going about doing good in this world. The first would be the case of a being too unsusceptible of education, too stupidly insensible of the treatment he received, to be diverted from gratifying a blind incli-

* *Political and Moral Essays*, pp. 253-255.

nation that he had to make himself agreeable and profitable to others,—a being that would exercise among men a genial and healthy influence, as a tench is said to do amongst fishes, without understanding. Such a being, though useful, would not be morally good, nor would his utility be of the highest order; indeed he would be scarcely human. Secondly, we may conceive a man, possessed of such a lively and ever actual insight into the paramount excellence of doing good, that he would no more think of failing to do good in seasonable circumstances, notwithstanding any perverse training or harsh treatment that he might have undergone, than we should think of cutting off our heads to appease our hunger. This man's will would not be free to turn away from doing good. At the same time he would be a moral agent, as distinguished from a physical one, for he would act with an appreciation of what he did. His would be a case of an intellectual necessity, similar to the necessity under which GOD and the angels and saints are of being holy, from seeing the clear vision of the beauty of holiness. Brute necessity, on the other hand, is the state of an agent that must act, without knowing what it does. Brute necessity is incompatible with either moral excellence or turpitude: intellectual necessity is incompatible with moral evil, but quite compatible with moral good.

A human being, lying under a brute necessity of evil doing, may be discussed in three shapes. In the first place, he may do evil from stupidity, not meaning what he does: but then it is no moral evil. Mill

seems to have wished to exclude this case by his phrase
"active in evil-doing." Secondly, we may speak of
"an original perversity of nature," that intends known
evil with a resistless necessity from the first. Such a
being would not be of sound mind: would be what is
called a "criminal lunatic"; and his actions, horrible of
themselves, would not be morally evil in him. Lastly,
we may conceive human beings with their wills set in
wickedness, whence no motive can convert them, not,
however, created in this state, but having come to it
by their own abuse of their free will. Such men would
be in the state and condition of devils. Of the devils
St Thomas writes, "The evil angels sin mortally in all
things whatsoever they do of their own will,"* and
he assigns as a reason this property of angelic nature,
that when once an angel takes a decisive resolution,
his will becomes eternally fixed in the same: "The
free will of man is flexible one way and another both
before and after election; whereas the free will of an
angel is flexible before election, but not after."† Such
a life, however, we may venture to think, is not studded
and diversified with a multitude of distinct sins, but
is one long sin, the beginning of which was a free act,
albeit the continuance is a necessity. We see some
approximation to this state in a confirmed habit of vice
even in a man on earth.

* *Summa*, 1a 2æ, q. lxxxix, art. 4. † 1a, q. lxiv, art. 2.

XIV

"Real fatalism is of two kinds. Pure, or Asiatic fatalism,—the fatalism of the Œdipus, holds that our actions do not depend upon our desires. Whatever our wishes may be, a superior power, or an abstract destiny, will overrule them, and compel us to act, not as we desire, but in the manner predestined. Our love of good and hatred of evil are of no efficacy, and though in themselves they may be virtuous, as far as conduct is concerned, it is unavailing to cultivate them. The other kind, modified fatalism I will call it, holds that our actions are determined by our will, and our will by our desires, and our desires by the joint influence of the motives presented to us and of our individual character; but that, our character having been made for us and not by us, we are not responsible for it, nor for the actions it leads to, and should in vain attempt to alter them. The true doctrine of the Causation of human actions maintains, in opposition to both, that not only our conduct, but our character, is in part amenable to our will; that we can, by employing the proper means, improve our character, and that if our character is such that while it remains what it is, it necessitates us to do wrong, it will be just to apply motives which will necessitate us to strive for its improvement, and so emancipate ourselves from the other necessity: in other words, we are under a moral obligation to seek the improvement of our moral character. . . When we voluntarily exert ourselves, as it is our duty to do, for the improvement of our character, or when we act in a manner which,—either consciously on our part or unconsciously,—deteriorates it, these, like all other voluntary acts, presuppose that there was already something in our character, or in that combined with our circumstances, which led us to do so, and accounts for our doing so."

The interest of this interesting passage,—with which the previous passage, n. 5, the reply to the Owenite, should be compared,—lies in the affirmation that "not only our conduct, but our character, is in part amenable to our will." How so? That is the question the answer to which should light up Mill's whole position, and reveal the gulf, if any gulf there be, between him and that " Modified Fatalism " which he reprobates. This then is his reply or replies:

R. 1. " We can, by employing the proper means, improve our character."

The reply merits all praise from the libertarian point of view. It is quite true. But how is it consistent with " the true doctrine of the Causation of human actions," as laid down by Mill? To get that doubt solved, we are obliged to ask for an explanation of the terms of the reply received. What are the " proper means" by employing which we can improve our character? Mill replies as follows:

R. 2. " The proper means for improving our character are our own voluntary exertions."

This reply is gathered from the last sentence in the extract quoted: " When we voluntarily exert ourselves, as it is our duty to do, for the improvement of our character," etc. Again, an excellent reply, and, as it stands, conceived quite in a libertarian spirit. But this libertarian spirit Mill hastens to exorcise and cast out. For the sentence goes on: " These [voluntary exertions], like all other voluntary acts, presuppose that there was already something in our character, or in that combined with our circumstances, which led us to do so, and accounts for our doing so." Alas, alas, here we are back in the squirrel's cage, the vicious circle, from which Mill seems impotent to escape. By a singular method, which we may call Roundabout Fatalism, he derives our volitions from our character and circumstances, our character from our volitions and circumstances (one most important circumstance being no doubt that of heredity), and those volitions again from our character and circumstances. Then, except our character and circumstances cause and determine us so to do, we shall make no voluntary efforts for the improvement of our character. In what does this account differ from the "Modified Fatalism" which represents "our character having been made for us and not by us"?

The only way to strike a difference, and it is a direct and very true way, is by saying that although character and circumstances must concur to induce us to make voluntary exertions to improve our character, for we can do nothing without motives, and motives suffer a sort of refraction in the character upon which they impinge; nevertheless, it rests with us finally, having the motive for voluntary exertion, to act upon it or to let it drop void and ineffectual, and this is an alternative ultimately ruled, not by motive and character, but by our own personal self. But this a statement of free will; the direct contrary of that doctrine of the "causation of human actions," i.e., their physical determination, which Mill maintains.

"We are under a moral obligation," writes Mill, "to seek the improvement of our moral character." This may be accomplished by "voluntary exertions"; but, as we have seen, those voluntary exertions are determined by that very character which needs them for its improvement. Should the character not be responsive to the need, Mill provides another remedy. "If our character is such that while it remains what it is, it necessitates us to do wrong, it will be just to apply motives which will necessitate us to strive for its improvement"; which means that we may be justly punished to set us on the way of reform. Here is a duty which we cannot do until we are punished for not doing it; a moral obligation, the fulfilment of which rests with the strong arm of the law that grips us. Awaiting that, we lie like over-turned motor cars, helpless for all good on the wayside of life. It is difficult to see any moral obligation in such a position of necessity.

Disagreeing with Mill in many things, I have never ceased to cherish for him a certain admiration. Since I first opened his pages, nearly forty years ago, I have ever admired his clear, incisive thought, his logical acumen, and his candour, shining out, as it often does, at the expense of his consistency. He is too ingenuous, too adverse to fatalism, too great a lover of individualism and liberty, to be a thorough determinist. In all this he forms a strong contrast to Hobbes, who drives his necessarianism, as he drives every other point of his grim philosophy, steadily and remorselessly to the final conclusion.

The difference between determinism and fatalism is not so much in theory as in practice. The fatalist acts upon his theory, and either sits idle in the absence of strong emotion, or surrenders himself to the impulse in which he recognises his destiny. The determinist, in England at least, shuts his determinism up with his books; and, in active life, uses his free will vigorously. Whatever academicians may say, an illogical escape into the realms of truth is preferable to detention in the logical bonds of error once entered upon. Thus escaping, on the whole we prosper in England, notwithstanding much bad philosophy.